BERLITZ®

SEVILLE

By the staff of Berlitz Guides

How to use our guide

- All the practical information, hints and tips that you will need before and during the trip start on p. 103.
- For general background, see the sections The City and the People, p. 6, and A Brief History, p. 12.
- All the sights to see are found on pp. 24–79. Our own choice of most recommended sights is flagged by the Berlitz traveller symbol.
- Entertainment, shopping, sports and fiestas are described on pp. 80–96, while information on restaurants and dining out can be found on pp. 97–102.
- Finally, at the back of the book you'll find a handy index, pp. 126–128.

Found an error or an omission in this Berlitz Guide? Or a change or new feature we should know about? Our editor would be happy to hear from you, and a postcard would do. Be sure to include your name and address, since in appreciation for a useful suggestion, we'd like to send you a free travel guide. Write to: Berlitz Publishing S.A., Avenue d'Ouchy 61, 1006 Lausanne, Switzerland.

Although we make every effort to ensure the accuracy of all the information in this book, changes occur incessantly. We cannot therefore take responsibility for facts, prices, addresses and circumstances in general that are constantly subject to alteration.

Text: Ken Bernstein
Photography: Claude Huber
Layout: Doris Haldemann
Staff Editor: Eileen Harr-Kyburz
We would like to thank Sr. José Rodríguez Castillejo of Seville for his help in the preparation of this book.
Cartography: 🅵🅰🅻🅺 Falk-Verlag, Hamburg

Contents

The City and the People

At once spiritual and sensual, Seville excels at the spectacular: flamenco, the bullfight, awesome religious processions, and those sultry Andalusian beauties with flashing black eyes.

The birthplace of Velázquez and Murillo, headquarters of the Conquistadores and the Inquisition, Seville is altogether as theatrical and grand as an opera. Certainly the city has inspired more than its share of grand opera: *The Barber of Seville, the Marriage of Figaro, Don Juan, Fidelio, Carmen...* A life-size statue of Carmen in a frilly dress loiters across from the bullring. Or you can visit the sweatshop where the temptress worked, rolling cigars on her thigh.

The city has many faces—Moorish and Christian, stately boulevards and narrow alleys, tranquil gardens as fragrant as jasmine, and cafés as noisy as an argument. But they're all parts of the heart and soul of Spain. With a population of 650,000, Seville is the fourth largest but most Spanish of the nation's cities.

The rest of Spain may have loosened its bonds with the Catholic church but the capital of Andalusia remains remarkably fervent in its faith. You're never more than a two-minute walk from a church. Chances are it's several hundred years old, and crammed with works of art, though it may be open only for mass. The Cathedral of Seville, one of the biggest churches in the world, is also one of the best endowed with old masters and priceless relics; many go all but unnoticed in dimly lit chapels. Alongside the cathedral soars a 12th-century tower with no competition on the whole skyline. Not only is the Giralda by far the tallest structure in town, it's also the most beautiful.

But beauty in Seville tends to a more intimate scale: a trickling fountain cooling a tiled patio, windowboxes of geranium overhanging a narrow lane, bougainvillea cascading down a whitewashed wall. It's a low-rise city so you won't have to crane your neck, just keep your eyes open.

Many of the world's great cities—think of London, Paris, Rome, Moscow and New York—were established along-

Beneath a street-corner shrine, a motorbike enthusiast shatters the siesta's silence in old Seville.

side rivers, the highways of ancient civilizations. Seville belongs to the Río Guadalquivir, the lifeline of Andalusia, which flows from the high sierras to the Gulf of Cádiz. Oceangoing ships can reach Seville from the Atlantic, about 96 kilometres (60 miles) to the southwest. Geography spells destiny.

Thus it was that the Phoenicians sailed up the Guadalquivir three thousand years ago to found a trading post where Seville stands today. The Romans who followed left many more traces hereabouts, starting with roads, aqueducts and amphitheatres; they also planted their language, their laws, and, eventually, Christianity. But the most profound foreign influence came from the Moors, whose blitzkrieg invasion of Andalusia reached Seville in A.D. 712. Under Muslim rule the city (called Ixbilya) prospered as a political capital and cultural centre for more than five centuries.

In 1248 the Christian forces led by King (Saint) Ferdinand III reconquered Seville. Much of the beauty the Moors had created was preserved,

even embellished, and the city's intellectual enterprise expanded.

A glorious new chapter began with the Columbus mission of 1492. Cashing in on Spain's Golden Age of discovery and colonization, Seville enjoyed exclusive rights to trade with America and became Spain's

In a flurry of faith, pilgrims set forth from Seville's great Gothic cathedral, begun in 15th century.

8

leading port and most densely populated city. As they used to say, "Madrid is the capital of Spain but Seville is the capital of the world." Columbus, by the way, spent a lot of time in and around the city, and Seville's Cathedral claims to be his last resting place. You can't miss the sarcophagus fit for a king, just inside the south entrance.

Everywhere you go in Seville, multiple layers of history unfold. The palace called the Royal Alcázar achieved its perfection under the 14th-century King Peter I (the Cruel). But this only elaborated on an existing Moorish citadel, built atop

Roman ramparts designed, it's suggested, by Julius Caesar himself. Some of the churches are recycled mosques, with minarets now belfries calling Christians to worship.

History also explains contemporary customs. Since the 16th century, the most solemn week in the Christian calendar has been the occasion for tremendous manifestations in Seville. The *Semana Santa* (Holy Week) processions fill the streets with masked penitents in pointed hoods, ornate candle-lit altars carried on the shoulders of the faithful, and spontaneous outpourings of plaintive music reminiscent of a muezzin's call to prayer.

Soon after the pageantry and fervour of Holy Week, Seville drops everything for the *Feria de Abril* (April Fair). What started in the 13th century as a cattle market developed into Andalusia's most colourful party, a kaleidoscope of flamenco, bullfights, horses, flowers and wine. Hundreds of thousands of people spend a gracefully sleepless week celebrating beauty, friendship, love, and the arrival of spring.

Parties aside, the best season to visit Seville is springtime. The orange trees lining the streets are in blossom, exuding a whiff of paradise. In May,

temperatures average a delightful 19 °C (66 °F). (The climate is similar in cheery October.) But come summer and it gets so hot even the locals wilt. After all, Seville is about as far south as Athens, and it suffers a chronic shortage of sea or mountain breezes. The altitude recorded at the town hall is a lowly 9.1 metres (30 feet). The average daily temperature in August hits 27 °C (about 81 °F), meaning an average daily *maximum* of 36 °C (97 °F). Even that's cool compared to the all-time high, a hellish 49 °C (120 °F). The other side of the coin is more reassuring: winters are rarely cold; frost is almost unknown.

Unless you're laid low by a summer heatwave, prepare for some energetic sightseeing. Not just the churches, monasteries and museums—including the best art hoard in Spain after the Prado. You'll want to wander the streets of some of the distinctive neighbourhoods, like the typical Santa Cruz district with its maze of narrow streets, and Triana, the old gypsy quarter across the river (the locals insist on calling themselves Trianeros, not Sevillanos). Irresistible, too, is the pedestrian zone in the historic centre of the city, radiating from Calle Sierpes, the traditional shopping street. Here they sell folding fans, Rococo religious images, even genuine flamenco dresses—and not just for the tourists. You can vary the sightseeing: take a boat trip, or a horse-and-carriage.

If you can be in Seville between April and October of 1992 you'll find the centre of gravity shifted across the river to the island of La Cartuja. There Expo '92 will mark the 500th anniversary of the New World connection, celebrating the Age of Discovery, past, present and future. When the festivities have ended, the city will count the bills—and the benefits, starting with long-overdue transportation and communications networks. And the island itself will be dedicated to education and research.

Anywhere you roam in Seville, handy outdoor cafés offer respite for tired feet and sensory overload. Life in general is more of an outdoor affair here than in most places, thanks to the climate and the gregarious nature of the people. Watch the early-evening promenade of elegantly dressed citizens with their peram-

Fashion-conscious matrons chat in Seville's chic shopping zone.

bulated babies. The window-shopping and chatting is interrupted from time to time by a snack and a beer or sherry. "Snack" is really an inadequate translation for the hot and cold *tapas* served at specialist bars all over town, anything from olives to marinated fish to meatballs. At peak hours *tapa* bars are always mobbed, but that's part of the fun.

And it goes on later than you're probably accustomed to. Dinner in the land of *gazpacho* and *pescaíto frito* (fried fish) is almost unthinkable before 10 p.m. and the night stays young for several more hours of festivity.

After you've seen Seville, branch out into Andalusia. The ancient Roman "digs" of Itálica are only minutes away. A daytrip through bull breeding country takes you to the underpopulated beaches of the Atlantic coast or the wine-and-horses town of Jerez and the nearby "white villages". Or head east to sunny Carmona, even sunnier Écija, and on to Córdoba, and the most wonderful mosque in Christendom.

Make your own itinerary, as intense or light-hearted as you please. Although time is bound to run out, relaxed but zestful Seville makes it feel as if there's always *mañana*.

A Brief History

A band of monumental heavyweights helped fashion the history of Seville. The roll call: Julius Caesar, King (Saint) Ferdinand III, Peter the Cruel, and even, if you believe the legend, the heroic Hercules. Tracking down the part Hercules might have played takes us into the nebulous realm of mythology, but this doesn't inhibit the locals. They proudly claim him as the founder of their town, first known as Hispalis.

Flesh-and-blood pioneers were the far-ranging Phoenicians, who sailed up the Guadalquivir river, a pleasant detour from Atlantic storms. Perhaps three thousand years ago they established an import-export base at the site of the future Seville. Their trading partners were some intriguing indigenous people, the Tartessians (mentioned in the Bible). Although the Tartessians devised a written language, it has never been decoded. But a wonderful sample of their handiwork is on show at Seville's archaeological museum.

Several centuries after the Phoenicians, the settlement was captured by an army of mercenaries in the employ of the Carthaginians, the era's most ambitious international businessmen. After that, little was heard of Tartessian civilization, which seemed to simply vanish.

Recorded history hereabouts begins in the 3rd century B.C. with dispatches from Punic War II. The Roman Empire was fighting Carthage for control of the Iberian peninsula, not to mention domination of the western world. Near present-day Seville, Roman forces commanded by the brilliant General Scipio the Elder won a climactic battle at Ilipa (now Alcalá del Río). The date was 206 B.C., four years before Scipio was to take on Hannibal himself in the battle of Zama in North Africa. Scipio won the big one, and henceforth was honoured as Scipio the African. (According to the historian Pliny the Elder, Scipio had another distinction: he was the first Roman to bare a freshly shaven face every day. That would have endeared him to all the future barbers of Seville.)

Roman Spain

Even as mopping-up operations were underway, the Romans founded a rest-and-relaxation facility for the legionnaires a few kilometres north of Seville. They named the place Itálica, and it grew into a key colonial centre. Itá-

lica was to go down in history as the home town of two celebrities—the Roman emperors Trajan and Hadrian.

In 45 B.C. Julius Caesar, no less, upgraded old Hispalis into a Roman municipality named Colonia Julia Romula. Meanwhile, nearby Itálica was booming; you can see the extent of its success by wandering among the sprawling ruins today: the amphitheatre was one of the largest in the empire.

Spain (the Romans called it Hispania) was divided into three provinces. The province of Baetica, covering roughly the territory of modern Andalusia, had its capital at Córdoba. The natives were so submissive that occupation forces were unnecessary; the province was assigned to civilian control. Soon everyone could understand Latin, and Christianity spread across the country. The Romans also bestowed on their subjects the tangible benefits of their culture, such as amphitheatres, aqueducts, baths and bridges.

As the Roman empire declined and the Dark Ages unfolded, the good times ran out for Seville. At the beginning of the 5th century the itinerant Vandals arrived and, as was their wont, sacked the city. Incidentally, one theory suggests that the name Andalusia derives from *Vandalusia*. If true, it would have been one of the Vandals' most positive contributions to the march of civilization. But "Andalusia" is generally thought to have come later, from the Arabic *al-Andalus*, meaning "the western land".

The Muslim Conquest

In A.D. 711 Arab-led Berber troops invaded Andalusia from across the strait in North Africa. The Moors or *moros* (as North African Muslims are usually called in Spanish history) strode northward on the good, straight roads the Romans had considerately built. They seized

Seville in 712, named it Ixbilya, and turned the city into a showcase for Islamic culture, as esoteric as poetry and song, as practical as irrigation techniques that made the orange trees bloom. (But Muslim Seville suffered a big setback in 844 when the Vikings, of all unexpected predators, sailed up the Guadalquivir with 16,000 troops and captured the city; after destroying many mosques and civic buildings they were expelled.)

The Moors went on to occupy most of Spain as far north as the Pyrenees. They stayed for centuries, leaving cities and forts and permanent traces on the peninsula's landscape. Their legacy is obvious, as well, in the people's faces and character.

Seville was ruled from Córdoba, headquarters of an independent caliphate. Soon internecine warfare broke out between clans, cliques and factions loyal to various Moorish leaders. Around the turn of the 11th century the caliphate splintered into tiny independent kingdoms called *taifas*. The *taifa* of Seville, ruled by the poet-prince al-Mutamid, was rated one of the richest and best organized societies in Muslim Spain.

By this time, though, the Christian Reconquest of Spain was pushing boldly into the heartland of the Moors. Al-Mutamid called for help from North Africa, from puritanical

Itálica mosaics and stately pines recall glories of ancient Rome. **15**

Berber zealots called the Almoravids. They not only helped, they grabbed control of Andalusia, only to be ousted by the next army of "helpful" tribesmen, the Almohads. Under the Almohad caliph, Abu Yaqub Yusuf, Seville entered its pre-Columbian golden age as the capital of Muslim Spain. The sultan sponsored an imposing public works program crowned by a minaret so tall and beautiful that the Christian forces, when they finally arrived, couldn't bring themselves to tear it down. It's called La Giralda.

The Reconquest

In the mid-13th century, King Ferdinand III of Castille and León led the Christian Reconquest of Andalusia. The middle-aged medieval crusader was famously successful in routing the Moors, who had, in any case, become altogether less fierce over the centuries of the occupation. Pope Clement X had the king sanctified in 1671; call him San Fernando.

The Christian liberation army entered Seville in November, 1248, after a terrible siege of nearly two years. Having captured the city, Ferdinand settled down and invited Castilian immigrants to do the same. They took over the property abandoned by thousands of residents who had fled to the last Muslim bastion, Granada. The saintly king, who died four years later in Seville, is buried in the cathedral.

Ferdinand's brainy son, Alfonso X (The Wise), turned Seville into something of an intellectual hothouse, recruiting a huddle of historians, scientists and translators. As a politician, though, the king was much less successful. He lost most of his kingdom to rival nobles led by his son, Sancho IV. Only Seville stayed loyal. A grateful Alfonso coined the emblem NO8DO; you'll see the logo in your travels around the town—on the façade of the City Hall, on the backs of buses, and even on manhole covers. NO8DO is a rebus reading "No-madeja-do", a sort of pun meaning "Didn't abandon me".

In the mid-14th century King Peter I (the Cruel) contributed priceless beauty to Seville. He hired the Mudéjar artisans who made the Alcázar what it is today—an oriental palace any king would love to live in. As for the epithet "cruel", some

El Rocío pilgrims hail Virgin of the Dew, rescued at Reconquest.

16

might consider it a mite harsh. Friends called him Peter the Just. Except for abandoning a couple of his brides, his unkindness was limited to staging some routine political assassinations. He might have done more to earn the title, but his career ended abruptly when he was 35 years old—his brother slew him.

Age of Discovery

In 1492, a year that shook the world, Spain was at the epicentre of the earthquake. Everything seemed to happen at once. Ferdinand and Isabella, the Catholic Monarchs, captured the jewel of the Muslim occupation, Granada, winning the final victory of the Reconquest. In the same year they acted on the advice of the Inquisitor-in-Chief, Tomás de Torquemada, and expelled all the Jews from Spain—at least those not already converted to Christianity or burned at the stake. (The Spanish Inquisition lasted three centuries in Seville, from the first group *auto-da-fé* in 1481 to the last flaming victim, an alleged witch, in 1780.)

But in 1492 the big event was the Columbus venture. The navigator from Genoa, sailing under Spanish sponsorship, brought back tidings of the New World—great news for Seville, the first city to welcome him back. Thanks to its strategic location and port facilities, Seville won the commercial jackpot: an exclusive franchise for transatlantic trade. Soon hordes of mariners and adventurers arrived hoping to sign up for a share of the action. Some would return laden with gold and pricey spices, others empty-handed but with a new view of the world. Many perished at sea or in hostile climes.

After cornering the market on trade with America, Seville enjoyed a couple of centuries of expansion and high living. Among the distinguished buildings attesting to the city's status at that time are the City Hall, the elegant Pilatos House, and what used to be the nerve centre of the American adventure—now the Archive of the Indies. And the converted minaret, the Giralda, got its bell tower. Seville's high society was invited to the 1526 wedding of Charles I and Princess Isabel of Portugal, who honeymooned in the Alcázar. Four years later Charles was crowned Holy Roman Emperor. He fought many wars on behalf of his far-flung interests, using mostly Spanish troops as cannon-fodder.

The ailing emperor abdicated in favour of his only son, Phi-

They Sailed from Seville

The Italian explorer Amerigo Vespucci (1454–1512) got his taste for adventure in Seville. He was working for a shipping company in the city when Columbus first made headlines. Vespucci abandoned his desk job and signed on for the first of four expeditions into the unknown. His claim to fame is not any territorial discovery but his understanding that the New World was a continent, not just scattered islands or a part of Asia. In Vespucci's honour the continent was named America.

Seville was also the base for Ferdinand Magellan (c. 1480–1521), the Portuguese navigator who led the first round-the-world expedition. To the horror of his countrymen, he sailed under the flag of Spain. (And he left a Spanish wife and child in Seville.) After discovering the Strait of Magellan at the southern tip of South America, his fleet crossed the Pacific. Only one of his five ships made it back to civilization, but that was enough for Magellan to win the circumnavigation prize—posthumously, as it happened. He was killed by unfriendly natives in the Philippines.

lip II, in 1556, amid hopes for an era of peace and prosperity. But Philip became over-confident and, for religious, political and personal reasons, sent the Spanish Armada to make war against England. He shouldn't have done it. Britannia proved that it ruled the waves; in fact, the English devastated the Spanish fleet without losing a single ship of their own.

The pious Philip III, who succeeded his father, did Andalusia no favour when he expelled the *moriscos*, descendants of Muslims who had converted to Christianity. The edict, in 1609, effectively deprived the region of some of its hardest-working farmers and artisans. During the reign of his lacklustre son, Philip IV, Spain lost the Thirty Years' War. Seville then suffered a crippling setback: an epidemic of bubonic plague in the late 1640s halved the city's population. Whole neighbourhoods were abandoned. Not only did grass grow in the streets, it grew more than a metre tall.

But 17th century Seville had its moments of glory, mostly on a cultural and artistic level. Cervantes began his manuscript of *Don Quixote* in the tranquillity of the local jail. In rather nicer surroundings in Seville, three of the world's greatest painters—Velázquez, Murillo and Zurbarán—first showed their genius. **19**

Seville on the Skids

The War of the Spanish Succession (1701–14) cost Spain much of its dwindling empire, specifically Belgium, Luxembourg, Milan, Sicily and Sardinia. Seville had already tightened its belt, with the transfer of the New World Fleet headquarters to Cádiz. In 1717 the mercantile exchange went there, too.

Good news was scarce in the 18th century. The most significant economic advance was the construction of Seville's tobacco factory, which was destined to contribute to the local colour in *Carmen*. It was, and is, one of the biggest buildings in Spain.

During the Napoleonic wars, Spanish ships fought alongside the French fleet in the battle of Trafalgar, near Cádiz. The British, this time under Admiral Lord Nelson, won the day, inflicting another naval disaster on Spanish pride.

Alliances changed suddenly, barely three years after Trafalgar, when Napoleon invaded Spain and installed his brother Joseph as King José I. French troops occupied Seville, which became sufficiently pacified for a gala visit by the interloper, who bedded down in the Alcázar. But the Spaniards finally overthrew the Bonaparte regime, with help from the

How to Write a Best-Seller

When he was a teenager, Miguel de Cervantes Saavedra (1547–1616) was sent to a Jesuit school in Seville. By the time he returned to the city in 1585 he'd been around: wounded in action at the Battle of Lepanto, then held captive for five years by North African pirates. After his liberation he hoped for some reward for services rendered. All he got was a thankless government job. He was assigned to an office in Seville requisitioning grain and olive oil for the Invincible Armada. His efforts grated on some of his reluctant "clients"; he was even excommunicated. But the worst was ahead. The auditors accused him of bookkeeping hanky-panky (they were mistaken, it was later admitted) and he landed in the royal jail in Sierpes Street. There, uncomfortably ensconced in the heart of old Seville, he began writing the world's most widely translated book (after the Bible) and best-selling novel of all time, *Don Quixote*.

Duke of Wellington. The whole 1808–14 saga is known as the Peninsular War, but in Spain it's called the War of Independence. Several South American colonies took advantage of the home country's distractions to revolt and abandon the shrinking empire. The remaining colonies, from Cuba to the Philippines, were lost in the Spanish-American War of 1898.

On the home front, 19th-century Seville started to take on a modern mien. Parks and gardens were laid out, the Triana bridge built, a bullfighting school established. Gaslight first brightened the streets in 1845, a couple of years before the arrival of the railway.

Years of Conflict

With Spain looking on from the camp of the neutrals, World War I killed about 8½ million people. But social unrest in Spain brought domestic violence; and any lingering complacency was snuffed out in its long war against Moroccan tribes.

A strongman, General Miguel Primo de Rivera, took over, with little support from the governed in spite of an ambitious public works budget. Among his last gestures was the Great Iberoamerican Exhibition of 1929 in Seville, of which Plaza de España and a couple of classic five-star hotels are lasting souvenirs. The year is better remembered for the Wall Street crash, and the tidal wave of recession that deluged Spain, as well. Still, that doesn't explain the delay in paying off the deficit of Expo-29, which wasn't cleared up until 1988.

Primo was soon abandoned by the army and the crown. When republicans swept city elections in 1931, King Alfonso XIII, tarnished by his early support of the dictatorship, went into exile.

Under the new Republic, bitter ideological conflicts divided political parties and factions, and the church was also involved. Finally, in 1936, a large section of the army under General Francisco Franco rose in revolt against the left-wing Popular Front government. On Franco's side were monarchists, conservatives, the church and the right-wing Falangists (Spanish Fascist Party). Against him was a squabble of republicans, liberals, socialists, communists and anarchists.

Seville was the first city to fall to the rebels, in a brilliant coup by one of the Franco plotters, General Queipo de Llano. The capture of Radio Seville gave Queipo a powerful propaganda tool, which he used with panache.

The Civil War developed into a great 20th-century Cause, with support for both sides coming from outside Spain. Many Europeans saw it as a do-or-die confrontation **21** between democracy and dictatorship—or, as a choice between law and order or chaos and social revolution. With atrocities on both sides, the bloodshed lasted for three years, and cost hundreds of thousands of lives. The sober, wily Franco emerged as *caudillo* (leader) of a shattered postwar Spain.

The Road to Europe

After the war the hardship continued. But Franco eluded Hitler's embrace and kept Spain from combat in World War II. In the years following, though, the government was ostracized by the United Nations and foreign opinion was very hostile as Franco was considered the last

surviving dictator in Europe. Relations regularized in the fifties at the height of the Cold War when the tables turned and Franco was then seen as a hero of anti-communism. Spain was admitted to the United Nations in 1955, opening the gates to an unprecedented tourist invasion.

Two days after Franco's death in 1975 the monarchy was restored, in accordance with the *caudillo*'s wishes. King Juan Carlos surprised his handlers and the world and became Spain's helmsman on the road to democracy. The king's most heroic moment arrived in 1981 when he thwarted a military coup.

In the late 1970s and '80s most of the political relics were swept away. The Falange was wound down and the communists and socialists came out of the underground. (A youthful Seville lawyer, Felipe González, who had grown up in the clandestine socialist workers' party, was to become prime minister.) The church was disestablished. Divorce was legalized. Autonomy in varying degrees was granted to the regions. A new, democratic Spain joined NATO and the European Community. And on the eve of the fateful anniversary year of 1992, the nation—and Seville in particular—is looking back at its transatlantic destiny and ahead to its mission as a pillar of 21st-century Europe.

Sun-lover snoozes through history lesson in Plaza de España, built for Seville's 1929 world's fair. **23**

What to See

Sightseers prone to exhaustion should take Seville in small doses. The distances alone are impressive. Taxis and buses are the best way to get from one concentration of monuments to another; only the fearless or foolhardy would risk a self-drive tour through the clogged streets, anticlimaxing in the wretched quest for a parking space.

As it happens, several of the supreme sights rub shoulders in the historic centre of Seville, and that's where we start our survey. All the attractions can be approached in any order that suits your interests and timetable. The index at the end of this book will help you find any church or convent, palace or museum which may have eluded you.

Historic Heart

In 1401, a century and a half after the reconquest of Seville, the former Great Mosque was razed to make way for a colossal Gothic church. The city fathers ordered construction of a temple so big and beautiful that it would be unequalled, "even if future generations

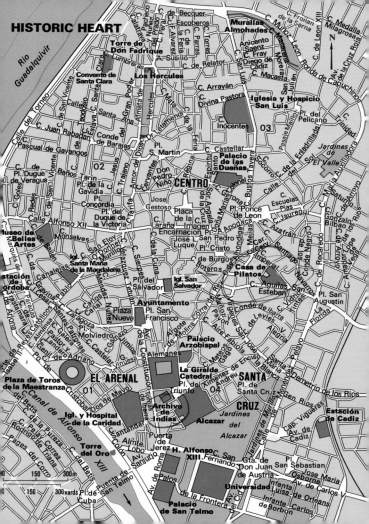

take us for madmen." It ended up the biggest cathedral in Spain and fourth biggest in the world—after Rome, London and Yamoussoukro (Ivory Coast). Stop-and-go construction, hampered by earthquakes, among other things, went on into the 20th century.

Tourists enter **La Catedral** through the neo-Gothic south portal, one of the newer elements of the building. You have to buy a ticket for a "cultural visit". (The cathedral is closed to sightseers on the major religious holidays, when the only way in is to infiltrate the crowds of worshippers.)

Just inside the south door, an ornate 19th-century **sarcophagus** is said to contain the remains of Columbus, well travelled even in death. He died in Valladolid in 1506 and was reburied in Seville. The rest of the posthumous journey is fogged by historical confusion, but the bones were shipped off to Santo Domingo and maybe Cuba. After the defeat in the Spanish-American War, his presumed remains sailed back to Seville, to be entombed in this ostentatious monument.

The cathedral's **main altarpiece** *(retablo mayor)*, closed off by an 18th-century grille, is so beautiful it's worth squeezing up against the screen for a good look. Generations of 15th- and 16th-century artists contributed to this enormous, golden bounty of sculptural details, showing action-packed biblical incidents. Facing this wonder is the **choir**, from the same era, with many additional uplifting illustrations intricately carved in the ebony choir stalls.

On opposite walls of the Plateresque **Capilla Real** (Royal Chapel), at the end of the central nave, are the tombs of Alfonso X (The Wise) and his mother, Beatrice of Swabia. A silver urn in front of the main altar contains the remains of Ferdinand III, liberator of Seville. Additional royal notables, including Peter the Cruel, are buried in the crypt below.

The elliptical **Sala Capitular** (Chapter House), in the southeast corner of the cathedral, is a gallery of artistic surprises, starting with the dome itself. It features an *Immaculate Conception* by Murillo, who also contributed eight saintly paintings on the walls. The adjoining anteroom houses an outstanding collection of choir books, starting with 15th-century illuminated works. In the **Sacristía Mayor** (Main Sacristy) hang

Cathedral and Orange Tree patio viewed from the Giralda Tower.

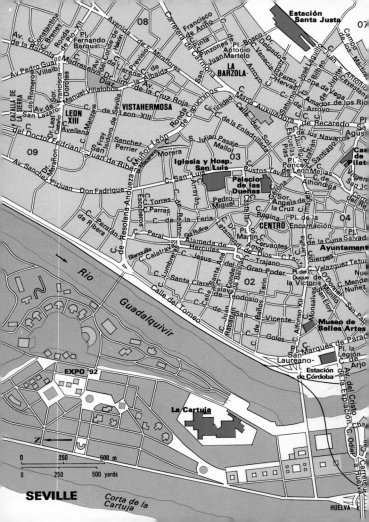

SEVILLE

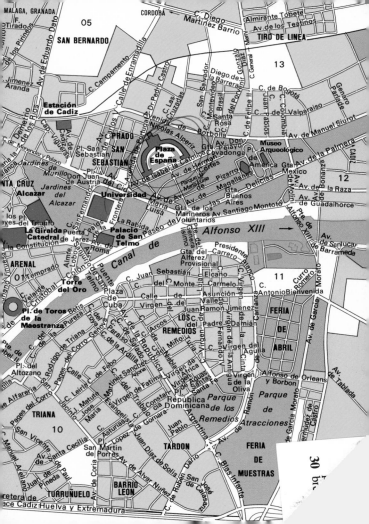

paintings by Luca Giordano, Murillo, Zurbarán and Pedro de Campaña. The cathedral holds more than 500 paintings in all, mostly in obscure side chapels; the artists range from anonymous 15th-century painters to Francisco de Goya, represented here by one of the few religious works he ever painted, *Saints Justa and Rufina*, two sisters who were to become Seville's first Christian martyrs. (On view in the Sacristy of the Chalices.)

A painting of the same two saints by Murillo is found in Seville's Fine Arts Museum. The canvas shows the sisters holding a miniature of the famous tower alongside the cathedral, called the **Giralda**, meaning weathervane. (The *g* is pronounced as a guttural *h*.) During an earthquake in 1504, legend has it, Justa and Rufina came down from heaven to steady the Giralda while all the buildings around were tumbling and crumbling. The weathervane, reaching nearly 100 metres (more than 300 feet) above the street, is the hollowed-out statue of a beautiful goddess representing the Triumph of Christianity, turning in the wind. You can hike up to the lookout level, stopping along the way for a rather and unusual views of

the cathedral's pinnacles and buttresses below and the cityscapes beyond.

The tower started out as a minaret, attached to the main mosque of Muslim Seville. In height and finesse it resembles two classic Moroccan minarets of the same era, at Marrakesh and Rabat. According to legend, the Muslim rulers negotiating the surrender of Seville in 1248 asked permission to destroy the mosque and minaret rather than let them fall into Christian hands. An appreciator of art, Prince Alfonso vetoed the proposal: "If one brick is removed from the tower they will all die under the knife." The brickwork, including the loveliest traceries and arches, is still intact.

The **Patio de los Naranjos** (Orange Tree Court) is the final element remaining from the original mosque. In this peaceful enclave the Muslims of Seville made their ablutions before entering the mosque. The fountain in the centre of the patio predates the Moorish invasion, though; the basin dates from the Visigothic era.

For a glimpse of Seville's Golden Age, see the Renaissance splendour of the **Archivo General de Indias** (Archive of the Indies)—on the opposite (south) side of the cathedral.

Architecture + Arabesques

One of Spain's most spectacular architectural styles is **Mudéjar**, the work of Muslim craftsmen employed by Christians after the Reconquest. A protected minority, these gifted artisans were renowned for blending Arabic and Spanish artistic forms. A notable example: ceilings decorated with three-dimensional geometrical intricacies, adding an Arabian Nights air to Peter the Cruel's Alcázar in Seville.

Non-Arab arabesques provide the frills in the 16th-century **Plateresque** style, named for its resemblance to the art of the silversmith *(platero)*. For the Plateresque architect, anything goes—medallions, fruit, flowers, faces—so long as it embellishes the façade of a church or palace, for instance Seville's Ayuntamiento.

Later, an even more florid style developed, called **Churrigueresque.** The name honours the Churriguera family, from Madrid, who devised everything from retables with flying angels to entirely sumptuous churches. Similar effusions were produced by Seville's Leonardo de Figueroa (1650–1730), especially the *San Telmo Palace.*

The architect was the great Juan de Herrera, designer of the monastery/palace of El Escorial, near Madrid. This building was the *Lonja*, commercial hub of the Spanish colonization programme, where 16th-century merchants divided up the newly discovered empire. Now it's a goldmine for scholars, the repository for all the papers of the era, from maps to invoices, documenting the development of the New World—some 90 million documents, now being computerized. Photocopies of the most precious items are for sale as souvenirs—for instance, a letter Columbus scrawled to his son, another from Amerigo Vespucci trying to clear up a little financial problem.

The Plaza del Triunfo, behind the Archives, celebrates no victory. "Triunfo" in this context refers to the monumental column in the middle of the square, recalling the earthquake of All Saints' Day, November 1, 1755. Much of Seville was damaged, but casualties were miraculously low, hence the monument of thanksgiving.

Whenever King Juan Carlos I comes to Seville, he unpacks his bags in the **Alcázar Real** (Royal Palace), as Spanish kings have been doing since the 13th century. But long before the Reconquest, this was the site of the ruler's palace, going back to the ancient Romans. You can enter the great walled Alcázar from Plaza del Triunfo via the **Puerta del León** (Lion's Gate), above which a 14th-century tile image of a lion symbolizes victory over the Moors. Just inside, we're told, 14th-century kings chained a live lion as a no-nonsense door-keeper.

The Alcázar's halls provide a concise if overpowering concentration of Mudéjar abandon—sumptuously decorated arches, walls, ceilings and floors produced by the Muslim artisans under the command of the Christians who had recaptured the city. A lovely example, the **Patio de las Doncellas** (Courtyard of the Ladies-in-waiting) is a perfect square surrounded by double marble columns. The royal princesses, cloistered upstairs, were able to peek out onto ceremonies below through their louvred windows.

Architecturally remarkable, the **Salón de Embajadores** (Ambassadors' Hall) is also known as the "hall of the half orange" *(la media naranja)*. The glittering 15th-century cupola, looks down on a fine marble floor.

In another part of the Alcázar, the **Palacio de Carlos V**

(Palace of Charles V), interest shifts from architecture to tapestry. The walls of one enormous hall are devoted to pictorial aspects of the Spanish conquest of Tunis, woven in Flanders but based on battlefield drawings.

Beyond the richly embellished salons and apartments of the Alcázar, the terraced **gardens,** scattered with pools and pavilions, sculptures and fountains, are superb in their own right. The Romans started the beautification here, planting cypress and laurel. But the big leap forward came during the Muslim period, when North African landscapers and gardeners added flowers and flowering shrubs and trees to charm the most demanding caliph.

Outside the Alcázar, the 18th-century building at Santo Tomás 5 would be worth visiting for its architectural value, even if it were empty. But they've named it the **Museo de Arte Contemporáneo** (Contemporary Art Museum) and filled it with the best of 20th-century Spanish art. The highlights tend to gravitate to the top floor. Some names to look

Giralda weathervane tops tallest, most beautiful building of Seville.

for: the Catalan Modest Cuixart, the satirical Valencian team of Rafael Solbes and Manuel Valdes and the Miró-esque Manuel Mompó, the sculptor Dario Villalba, and witty modern ceramics by Seville's Francisco Cortijo.

Santa Cruz Quarter

Bordering on the Alcázar, the Barrio de Santa Cruz contains the essence of picturesque old Seville. The whitewashed walls in this labyrinth of narrow—sometimes disconcertingly narrow—streets exude the fragrance of flowers, history, legend, and loads of charm. Fortunately for claustrophobes, the maze occasionally opens to reveal a plaza or gardened square.

Among the ways into the district, you can pass through the arch at the corner of the Patio de Banderas (bordering the Alcázar); or enter through the relaxing Murillo Gardens. This is not the sort of place to follow a specific itinerary; although the streets are well signposted, you could spend all your time consulting the map—and still

Whitewashed houses and flowers galore contribute to the special mood in the Santa Cruz district.

get lost. You'll see more if you just wander at will, peering into the patios as you pass. To help you get your bearings, though, here's an alphabetical checklist of some significant streets and squares:

Calle Fabiola. A plaque marks the birthplace (in 1802) of Nicholas Wiseman, a Catholic intellectual who became the first Archbishop of Westminster (London). He was burned in effigy there on Guy Fawkes Day, 1850.

Calle Jamerdana. Another plaque: the birthplace (in 1775) of José Maria Blanco White, who abandoned the Catholic priesthood for journalism, poetry and politics in Britain.

Calle Judería. One of the street names to remind us that this was the Jewish quarter.

Calle Santa María la Blanca. The church of the same name was built in 1391—as a synagogue. It contains a *Last Supper* by Murillo.

Calle Santa Teresa. Relics of St. Teresa in late 16th-century San José Convent, which she founded; opposite, Murillo House, in which the painter died, with his studio reconstructed and a number of worthy works of art on view. (Being restored.)

Callejón del Agua. Lovely gardened houses hide here,

Blue tile illustrations on façade of the Santa Caridad church, attributed to Seville's Murillo.

including one in which the hispanophile American writer Washington Irving once lived.

Plaza Doña Elvira. Thirteen big orange trees shade this distinguished square, once the theatrical heart of Seville.

Plaza de Refinadores. Note the bronze statue of fictional Don Juan, immortalized by Tirso de Molina, Molière, Mozart, etc.

Plaza de Santa Cruz. The French tricolor waves over this utterly charming Andalusian

priests. Its Baroque church is a treasure house of art works. (Closed for renovation.)

On the edge of the Santa Cruz district, Renaissance aristocrats with taste to match their wealth built a delightful Mudéjar monument, a sort of scaled-down Alcázar. The **Casa de Pilatos,** home of the Dukes of Medinaceli, surrounds a gorgeous patio featuring ancient statues a museum-keeper might swoon over. Niches around the patio contain the busts of notables such as Tiberius, Caligula, Hadrian—even Charles V (though not in a toga). Upstairs, for a separate admission charge, you can see family heirlooms, including a Goya bull-fight painting.

In Plaza de Pilatos, facing the house, a statue of Zurbarán shows the artist dressed as a knight with palette; unfortunately, his bronze paintbrush and sword were the victims of vandals.

square, marking the mansion occupied by the French consulate. The ornate wrought-iron cross in the centre of the plaza dates from the 17th century. Murillo was buried here.

Plaza de los Venerables. The *Hospital de los Venerables,* founded in the 17th century, was a nursing home for retired

Toward the River

The Latin motto over the main door of the **Hospital de la Santa Caridad** (Holy Charity Hospital) says *Domus pauperorum scala coeli* (Poorhouse, stairway to heaven). If you have to go to the poorhouse, you could scarcely do better than enrol- **37**

ling here. You'd be surrounded by priceless works of art.

The institution was founded by Don Miguel de Mañara, a 17th-century playboy who turned to philanthropy; his statue stands in the garden across the street, where the hospital's pensioners grow flowers to sell for pocket money. The highlight of Santa Caridad is its church. The main **altar** is a gold dazzle with soaring angels and swirling spiral columns, and the walls are lined with **paintings** by Murillo. Another painting greatly admired here is a desperately symbolic *Finis gloriae mundi* by a colleague of Murillo, Juan de Valdés Leal. On your way out of the church you'll see *reproductions* of four Murillo paintings now owned by museums from Ottawa to Leningrad. The originals, it is pointedly explained, were "pillaged" in 1810 by Napoleon's chief of staff, Marshal Nicolas-Jean de Dieu Soult. Incidentally, the splendid *azulejos* (painted tiles) on the façade of the church are attributed to Murillo, too.

Spanish cities tend to locate their bullrings on the edge of town, but not Seville. The huge, whitewashed stadium dominates the avenue paralleling the waterfront, the Paseo de Cristóbal Colón—yet an-

other gesture to Columbus. The official name of the institution is **La Plaza de Toros de la Real Maestranza**, and it was built in 1760 in classical style. *Aficionados* unhesitatingly qualify it as the world's most beautiful bullring. Every bullfighter of note has fought here, and the very best have left the ring atop the shoulders of their adoring fans through the stately main gate.

Next door to the bullring is operatic Seville's new opera house, the **Teatro de la Maestranza**. With the biggest stage in Spain, it's designed for ballet and concerts as well as operas as grand as can be.

The 12-sided, 13th-century **Torre del Oro** (Golden Tower) is no longer sheathed in golden tiles, but it's still a handsome relic of Almohad times. From its riverside location you might take it for a watchtower. But it had an added role. Every day at dusk the Moors stretched a heavy chain from the Torre del Oro to a tower on the opposite bank to keep out amphibious invaders. Finally, in 1248, a brilliant Spanish admiral, Ramón de Bonifaz, employed

Enveloped in frothy frills, bows and ribbons, a doll-sized señorita of Seville is carried to a fiesta.

Operatic Capital

Everybody with a Spanish connection, from Columbus to Quixote, seems to have inspired an opera. Seville is the favourite setting. For starters (in chronological order):

Mozart's *Marriage of Figaro* introduces the wheeler-dealer valet who outwits his employer, owner of a castle near Seville. The story line comes from the French playwright and adventurer Beaumarchais.

A specific unprincipled nobleman in Seville is said to have provided the model for the nasty seducer Don Juan, written about by Tirso de Molina and immortalized in Mozart's *Don Giovanni*.

Beethoven's *Fidelio* takes place in a very unsavoury prison fortress near Seville.

Rossini's *Barber of Seville* reassigns the characters of Figaro & Co. to a new plot. As usual, love conquers all.

Bizet's *Carmen*, the tragic story of the infatuated soldier and the gypsy temptress, was first told by the French writer Prosper Mérimée.

In the 20th century a less celebrated opera was set in Seville. Prokofiev's *Betrothal in a Monastery* is based on the comic opera *The Duenna* by the 18th-century Anglo-Irish dramatist Sheridan.

an armoured assault ship to break the chain and enter the port, opening the way to the reconquest of Seville. In the Golden Age the tower served as a vault for gold and silver shipments from the Indies, and later as a prison. You may be surprised to be met at the door by a sailor in uniform, selling tickets to the **museum** now housed in the tower. It's full of salty souvenirs, like old cannons and anchors, a diving helmet, model ships and full-sized tillers and figureheads.

Inland again, Seville's main street, Avenida de la Constitución, ends at **Puerta de Jerez**, now a traffic circle with a fountain in the middle; it once was a gate in the city wall. A small **chapel** in Gothic-Mudéjar style on the north side dates from the beginning of the 16th century. The Yanduoi palace next door was the birthplace of the poet Vicente Aleixandre (1898–1984). On the east side of the intersection, the monumental neo-Moorish building surrounded by palm trees is a celebrated hotel, the **Alfonso XIII**. Ever since 1928 it's been a second home for visiting princes, film stars and tycoons.

Seville's storied tobacco factory has moved. The big modern plant is across the river from the old one; if the breeze is right you can stroll the Paseo de las Delicias and smell a million virgin cigarettes. When the original **Real Fábrica de Tabacos** was built in the early 18th century it was the biggest building in all Spain after the Escorial. The 19th-century French author-traveller Théophile Gautier visited the factory and saw what it must have been like in Carmen's day: "Five or six hundred women are employed... They were talking, singing and arguing all at once. I've never heard such a din. They were mostly young, and there were some very pretty ones." The place still has its noisy moments, and pretty girls: it happens to be the main building of the University of Seville.

A final monumental building, next door to the University: the **Palacio de San Telmo.** The superstructure around the main entrance is an unrestrained exploit in Churrigueresque or Andalusian Baroque architecture from the 18th century. Featured among many statues is that of St. Telmo, patron saint of sailors, a hint of the building's original purpose as a school for sea captains. In modern times it has served as a seminary. (The building is closed at present for restoration.)

María Luisa Park

The María Luisa in question was Princess María Luisa of Orleans, Duchess of Montpensier. In 1893 she gave the city of Seville the nicest gift: part of the gardens of the San Telmo Palace, her home at the time. It was the start of a prodigious gardening project and a masterpiece of landscaping.

María Luisa Park is full of surprises and delights, contrasting colossal palms and eucalyptus with delicate almond trees and tentacular fig trees, alternating ceremonial promenades with intimate lanes. Then there are fountains, sculptures, grottos, even a little moat-bordered island with peacocks and less melodramatic birds in the trees.

With the world's fair of 1929 the park was "urbanized", but it's still overwhelmingly green. Some of the flamboyant buildings of the exposition are still in use as government offices, museums or foreign consulates. The centrepiece is **Plaza de España,** a vast semicircle bounded by a duck-infested canal with row boats for hire. The architectural ensemble embracing the plaza features a giant curved arcade decorated with the faces of dozens of great Spaniards, in chronological order from Seneca to **41**

Sorolla. Beneath are tableaux of historic events and maps of each province, from Álava to Zaragoza.

On opposite sides of the park's Plaza de America stand early 20th-century impressions of a Mudéjar palace and a Renaissance palace. The Mudéjar Pavilion houses the **Museo de Artes y Costumbres Populares** (Museum of Folk Arts and Customs). It concentrates on the colourful details of everyday life in old Andalusia with displays of farm implements, a wine press, a baker's oven, furniture, musical instruments, and folkloric costumes. (Closed for renovations.)

The Renaissance Pavilion contains Seville's **Museo Arqueológico** (Archaeological Museum), a sensational trove of local art works going back to cave-man days. Everything is the genuine article—except the pseudo-historic building itself. The exhibits are organized in chronological order, starting (in the basement) in the days when mammoth roamed Andalusia. There are Stone Age ceramics, Bronze Age idols carved of bone, illustrated gravestones and stelae.

Rooms 5 and 6 feature the wonders of the mysterious Tartessian civilization, called the **42 Carombolo Treasure.** It was unearthed in 1958 in a hill only three kilometres (two miles) from Seville. The highlights from the 6th century B.C., dramatically displayed in a burglar-proofed glass case, are 21 gold articles such as bracelets, plaques and a necklace. They are all adorned with tiny shields about the size of the modern 1-peseta coins. In the same room is the small statue of a long-haired goddess named **Astarté**, a seated figure with very ample breasts

and a certain smile. She now lacks one arm and one hand, but, then, she's about 28 centuries old.

Upstairs, the main floor emphasizes the Roman era, with giant **statues** from Itálica (only the bearded Emperor Hadrian is intact) and a vast mosaic from Écija showing two lions pulling a cart. A statue called the Hermes of Mars, from the 2nd century B.C., is considered Spain's finest example of classical sculpture.

Over the River

Inevitably, the Guadalquivir has lost some of its air of romance. Instead of galleons sailing forth for the New World, tourist excursion boats blare out peppy music and trilingual travelogues. And scull races and pedalo outings hardly

Brushing up on shades of green, artists depict María Luisa Park.

match the drama of approaching warships. One more prosaic detail: the river as seen from central Seville isn't really the Guadalquivir but a back-channel, stopped up to avoid seasonal inundations. (Flood-proofed, the diverted river is to be restored to its original course for the 1992 celebrations.)

From anywhere along the riverside promenade, for instance near the bullring or the Torre del Oro, there's an appealing view of the **Triana** district on the opposite shore, with its three- and four-storey houses painted in pastel shades. The name Triana may be derived from Trajan, the Roman emperor born in Itálica in A.D. 53. Triana was the traditional home of Seville's sailors, longshoremen and fishermen. Sea captains went to Triana to sign up rank and file mariners for the great expeditions to the western hemisphere. For centuries ferryboats shuttled between Triana and Seville, and there was a pontoon bridge, but in 1852 a cast-iron bridge, the **Puente de Isabel II**, provided the first secure fixed link. The easier contact failed to dilute the special character of Triana and the Trianeros, noted for their talent as flamenco singers and bullfighters. Another foundation of Tria-

na's fame: the district is built on clay, and it thrived as a centre of ceramics centuries ago. You can still find some attractive tiles, pots and figurines on sale.

On the Triana side of the bridge—actually *on* the bridge —a tiny **chapel** is dedicated to the *Virgen del Carmen*. The bridge leads into the Plaza del Altozano, most notable for a modern **sculpture** of the bullfighter Juan Belmonte, a local hero sometimes called "El

Pasmo de Triana'' (the marvel of Triana). In a dramatic affectation, the statue shows the matador disembowelled—or at least sunlight shines through his body. This is odd, for unlike many of his contemporaries, Belmonte avoided the ultimate goring and died at a ripe old 70.

On the opposite side of Plaza del Altozano, just off Calle de San Jorge, you can dip into some heady local colour at the **mercado** (market) of Triana. Rather than a covered market

A glass of tinto before the rush in a tapa bar near the cathedral.

it's a complex of outdoor stalls with overhanging roofs so close together the shopping is almost rainproof, or sunproof. Here they sell cockles, mussels, live prawns, and fresh fish as big as a mighty tuna or as tiny as mini-sardines; and daintily displayed fresh fruits and vegetables. The market occupies the site of the medieval Castle of Triana, **45** which housed the Tribunal of the Holy Inquisition. It was torn down in the 19th century, but the memory is preserved in the alley here signposted *Callejón de la Inquisición*.

The riverside street of Triana, **Calle Betis**, is a logical place for a stroll, punctuated by refreshment stops. The street is a hotbed of bars and restaurants. A visible bonus is the inspiring view back across the river to the skyline of Seville.

A couple of streets inland, the **Iglesia de Santa Ana** (St. Anne's Church) is considered very important for its early Gothic architecture. Some pleasant ceramics decorate the

top of the bell tower, and in the middle of the main altar, greatly admired sculptures of the Virgin and St. Anne are about as old as the church itself, founded by Alfonso X late in the 13th century.

In Calle Pureza (Purity Street), the **Capilla de los Marineros** (Sailors' Chapel) was a

special place for seamen bound for the Indies; they stopped here to say their final prayers before setting sail into the unknown. Restored in the 18th and 19th centuries, the chapel is now the home of one of Seville's best loved religious images, the *Virgen de la Esperanza de Triana*. The tearful Virgin, surrounded by gold and jewels, flowers and candles, is paraded through streets thronged with the faithful on Holy Thursday.

The next bridge southward, the **Puente San Telmo**, carries traffic across the river between two important junctions: Puerta de Jerez and Plaza de Cuba. Here begins the elegant boulevard called Avenida República Argentina, lined with tall palm trees and expensive high-rise blocks of flats. The ground floors are assigned to posh restaurants and boutiques, and an impressive number of banks. Avenida República Argentina is the main street of the very fashionable district called **Los Remedios**. On the edge of this quarter the Recinto Ferial (fairgrounds) is the site of the stupendous Seville April Fair (see page 94).

A curtain of sausages separates Triana vendors from the clients. **47**

Novel design enhances graceful span built for La Cartuja fair.

La Cartuja

A few hundred metres north of Triana, on the banks of the Guadalquivir, a Carthusian monastery (*La Cartuja* for short) was founded in 1400. The Carthusians were affiliated with the French Charterhouse monks, whose good works include the fabrication of an elixir, Chartreuse.

This monastery, Santa María de las Cuevas, was a favourite hangout of Columbus. Another historic footnote: Napoleon's invasion forces took over the monastery in 1810 and made it the southern headquarters of Marshal Soult. In an even more drastic turn of events 25 years later, Spain expelled the religious orders, including the hooded Carthusians. La Cartuja was con-

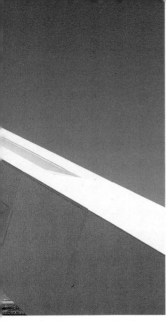

over the 538 acres (215 hectares) of the site chosen for the Seville Universal Exhibition of 1992, or **Expo 92**. All over the city, as well, there was upheaval as highways, bridges and tunnels were built. The municipality took out big newspaper ads apologizing for the "problems, traffic jams, noise, pollution, strains, discomforts, delays, machinery, fumes and slowness", but promising a glorious problem-free future after 1992.

The theme of the world's fair, running from April to October of 1992, is The Age of Discovery. By no coincidence, Expo coincides with the quincentenary of the Columbus expedition. The project clearly is the biggest thing to hit Seville since 1492. A few statistics:
Transport and infrastructure investment: 800,000 million pesetas (7 billion dollars).
Jobs created: 18,000.
Reforestation: 350,000 trees and plants.
Countries participating: 103.
Visitors anticipated: 18 million.
Parking space: 40,000 cars and 1,100 buses.

verted into a ceramics factory operated by a Liverpool firm, Pickman & Co. The enormous kilns, which explain the establishment's bizarre profile, were shut down as recently as 1982.

Between the 15th and 18th centuries, La Cartuja survived a number of devastating floods and three great earthquakes. But these disasters were trivial compared to the jolting changes that befell the island in the late 1980s. Workers and earth-moving behemoths swarmed

After the fair, Spain plans to continue to exploit the investment in La Cartuja—the highways, bridges, telecommunications facilities and some of the buildings. The island will be a **49** campus devoted to science and industry. It should be a favoured place to study or work, only minutes from the heart of Seville

The Columbus Connection

The monastery of La Cartuja played host to kings (Charles V, Philip II), a saint (Teresa of Ávila) and the Columbus family.

Christopher Columbus spent considerable time in residence. His contact and confidant was an Italian monk, Gaspar Gorricio; they maintained a long correspondence, which became essential to generations of scholars. Over a period of years Columbus used the monastery as a refuge, a source of spiritual renewal, and a place to store his books and papers.

Columbus died in Valladolid in 1506. His body was reburied in the crypt of the Chapel of Santa Ana in La Cartuja, where it was accounted for between 1509 and 1536. His remains thereafter were shuttled between Spain and Spanish America, ending up, it's believed, in the cathedral of Seville after the Spanish-American War. The Great Navigator's brother Diego, his son (another Diego) and other family members were also buried in La Cartuja.

yet much cooler in summer. Taking a tip from the Moors, the Expo designers combined vegetation, ventilation and evaporation to create a remarkably benign microclimate.

North of the Cathedral

Herds of municipal buses converge on **Plaza Nueva** (New Square), marked by an equestrian monument to King Ferdinand, liberator of Seville. (For years, temporary walls hiding much of the statue have constituted an ugly memorial to an underground fiasco: Plaza Nueva was a key construction site in a plan to build a subway system, but after much expensive tunnelling it was discovered that the city's subsoil was unfit to support such a project.)

Across Avenida de la Constitución from the plaza, Seville's **Ayuntamiento** (City Hall) is as stately as a coronation. But go round to the opposite side, on the Plaza de San Francisco, to fully appreciate the triumph of the elaborate Plateresque style, all pillars and arches and reliefs and medallions. Inside, as you'd expect, one public room is more magnificent than the next, with impressive ceilings, chandeliers and furnishings.

From city council meetings to formal receptions, the Ayuntamiento has been a classic setting ever since the 16th century. The archives bulge with papers documenting Seville's links with royal luminaries like Alfonso the Wise, Pedro the Cruel and Ferdinand and Isabella. (The building is closed for restoration until early 1992.)

The **Plaza de San Francisco,** where Seville's elite gather in reserved seats and boxes to watch the Holy Week processions, has a spectacular history. In the middle ages, crowds would assemble here for chivalric jousting competitions. Later, the square was the scene of the *autos-da-fé* during the Inquisition, when prominent heretics were burned at the stake to encourage the spectators to mend their ways. (The

Canaries are given an airing and audition at the Alfalfa market.

less notorious culprits were disposed of in private in the Triana headquarters of the witch-hunters.) Authorities disagree on the total number of victims during the three centuries of the Inquisition, but according to one historian 2,000 citizens went up in flames in a single year.

Calle Sierpes, Seville's most typical street, is rich in history and colour. The shops sell everything from rare antiques to collapsible fans, from elegant fashions to kitsch souvenirs—how about a model of the Giralda tower with sound and light effects? The tone changes every few doors on this pedestrians-only street of boutiques, cafés, bookstores and pinball-machine casinos. At the beginning of Calle Sierpes, on the bank building at No. 85, a **plaque** marks the spot where the Cárcel Real (royal prison) used to be. Cervantes did time here—long enough to start writing Quixote. Actually there are Cervantes plaques all over town, marking the places he wrote about. (A statue of the author is nearby, around the corner in a small gardened

In the pedestrian shopping area, neo-Moorish architectural ideas rise towards a marshmallow sky.

triangle in view of the city hall.) Everyone gravitates to Calle Sierpes—shoppers, businessmen, tourists, gypsy mendicants, lottery salesmen, pickpockets, country bumpkins and the shell-game conspirators who prey on them.

Just off Calle Sierpes, the **Capilla de San José** (St. Joseph's Chapel) is a refuge amidst all the hubbub. This lavish little 18th-century church brims with Baroque works of art, from the altar to the organ.

Like the Cathedral of Seville, the **Iglesia San Salvador** (Church of the Saviour), one street east of Calle Sierpes, was built on the site of a mosque. Inside the vast cruciform temple, the sumptuous Baroque altarpiece is as tall as a four-story building. The side entrance opens onto the original Muslim courtyard, the Patio de los Naranjos. Here, too, is the Capilla de los Desemparados (Chapel of the Homeless), a mini-chapel furnished with blue tiles and stucco, so small that half a dozen worshippers constitute a crowd.

West of Calle Sierpes, the **Iglesia de la Magdalena** is dedicated to Mary Magdalene, represented in an 18th-century woodcarving in the main altarpiece. Elsewhere in the three-aisled Baroque church are art **53** works by Zurbarán, Lucas Valdés, Pedro Roldán and others. Before this church was built there was a Dominican convent on the site.

Another former convent now contains the best art gallery this side of Madrid: on Plaza del Museo, Seville's **Museo de Bellas Artes** (Fine Arts Museum). (Most of the building has been closed for lengthy renovations.) The Baroque Convento de la Merced (Mercy Convent) was confiscated in 1835 when Spain cracked down on religious orders. The expropriation law not only provided a distinguished location for a museum, it also filled the institution with works of art suddenly acquired from other monasteries, creating a bumper collection of paintings, sculptures and applied art.

As you might expect, a high proportion of the works amassed bear on religious themes, but there's more: the portrait of his son Jorge Manuel by El Greco, or an earthy view of the *cigarreras* in Seville's legendary tobacco factory by Gonzalo de Bilbao. Outstanding foreign artists from Hieronymus Bosch and Rubens to Veronese and Titian are represented. But the big attraction for most visitors is the wealth of the **Seville School.**

Seville is one of a handful of European cities, such as Antwerp, Florence and Venice, to have spawned recognizable schools of art. The Seville School was founded, appropriately enough, by an art teacher. In the 17th century his students and their friends contributed to the brilliance of Seville's Golden Age.

The teacher was **Francisco Pacheco** (1564–1654), author of *The Art of Painting*, a book of tips on contemporary technique as well as biographies of some leading artists of the age. But as a creative artist this academician has gone down in history as no more than mediocre.

Pacheco's most famous pupil—and son-in-law—left his native Seville early in his career. Critics consider it a mercy that **Diego Velázquez** (1599–1660) left behind most of his teacher's strictures when he went to Madrid. Hired by Philip IV, Velázquez became an amazingly perceptive court painter and, quite simply, the greatest Spanish artist of the 17th century.

Another of Pacheco's students, **Alonso Cano** (1601–67),

Moody drama and piercing light by Seville School's Valdés Leal.

gained considerable fame as a painter and sculptor in spite of his hectic lifestyle. He was arrested on suspicion of murder (but freed) and for debt (but not freed); and he had a problem with the police in connection with a duel. His most impressive monument is the façade of Granada Cathedral.

A father and son from Seville helped to develop the Spanish Baroque style. **Francisco Herrera** the Elder (1576–1656) may have been an early teacher of Velázquez. His son, **Francisco Herrera** the Younger (1622–85), also made his reputation as a painter of dramatic religious scenes. He was one of the founders of a new Academy of Painting in Seville but left for Madrid, where he painted frescoes and royal portraits.

Francisco Zurbarán (1598–1664) is famed for his mastery of light and shade and the deep religious belief he conveys. His monks, priests and saints are dressed in flowing robes with almost tangible textures.

If Velázquez is best loved for his real-life portraits of pretty princesses and court dwarves, **Bartolomé Esteban Murillo** (1617–82) draws scorn for some of his lovable ragamuffins. His detractors use adjectives like "mawkish" and "saccharine" for his later work, but the

human element in Murillo's urchins, beggars and saints has won him lasting popularity.

A founder, with Murillo, of the Seville Academy, **Juan de Valdés Leal** (1622–90), produced some terrifyingly gory scenes. Wild lighting effects and violent action are characteristic, and seem to reflect his difficult personality. But he was a master of form, colour and narrative.

Perhaps it was the Andalusian climate, but the members of the Seville School enjoyed unusual longevity. As you'll see from the dates above, they lived, on average, 70 years.

More Churches and Convents

North of the Fine Arts Museum, a bit remote from the prime tourist attractions, an essentially working-class area contains historic churches and convents with legends to match.

A starting point is the **Alameda de Hércules,** the venue of a fascinating flea market every Sunday morning. They sell anything from genuine antiques to used hubcaps. The rest of the week the Alameda is a spacious avenue, much less fashionable than when it was the city's prime promenade. Towering

Towering Survivals

After the Christian Reconquest, churches in many Spanish cities were built on the ruins of mosques. In Seville they turned the minarets into belfries. The most beautiful case study is the Giralda, next to the Cathedral, but less celebrated examples are worth a look:

The **Omnium Sanctorum** church, east of the Alameda, has a belfry patterned on the Giralda. Note, too, the 13th-century Gothic-Mudéjar main portal.

Farther eastward, **Santa Marina** church, reconstructed in Gothic style in the 14th century, kept the minaret, simply adding bells.

The former minaret of **San Marcos** church is considered the most graceful tower in Seville after the Giralda. The main portal is also a beauty. At the start of the Civil War, leftwing firebrands sacked and burned all three churches.

One more minaret: **Santa Catalina** church, a 14th-century Mudéjar project, is protected as a national monument. The tower is one of several aspects of the original mosque still visible. But many changes have been wrought.

over the Alameda's treeline are a pair of columns said to have belonged to an ancient temple to Hercules. Atop these columns stand heroic statues of Hercules and Julius Caesar, who could be considered co-founders of Seville. The faces of the statues resemble Charles I and Philip II—poetic license, perhaps, or an artist toadying to his boss.

Between the Alameda and the river, the **Iglesia de San Lorenzo** (St. Lawrence Church) was founded in the 13th century. The five-aisled church is generously endowed with paintings and statues from the 16th and 17th centuries. Alongside San Lorenzo, the **Capilla de Nuestro Padre Jesús del Gran Poder** (Chapel of Jesus the Almighty) is a magnet for Seville's faithful. Its altar spotlights Seville's most beloved image of Christ, an early 17th-century statue of Jesus carrying the cross, by the sculptor Juan de Mesa. The weathered face is famous for its evocation of suffering and forgiveness. The elaborate processional float built around this image is one of the highlights of Seville's Holy Week.

Several streets northward, a peaceful, shady patio of orange trees leads to the **Convento de Santa Clara** (St. Claire's Convent). The Gothic-Mudéjar church, begun in the 15th cen-

tury, has fine ceilings and decorations. Adjoining is a curious square tower, the **Torre de Don Fadrique** (Prince Fadrique's Tower)—Gothic on top and Romanesque below. The prince was sentenced to death for plotting against his brother, Alfonso X (the Wise). But 13th-century gossips maintained that Fadrique was disposed of because of his love affair with the young widow of Fernando III, Juana of Ponthieu—his stepmother. Fadrique's Tower, ostensibly built as a watchtower but actually a lovenest, now embraces the municipal archaeological museum. (Closed for restoration.)

The Cistercian **Convento de San Clemente** (St. Clement's Convent), very near the river, was founded soon after the reconquest of Seville. The church has a fine Mudéjar coffered ceiling. Oustanding art works by Pacheco and Valdés Leal came later.

Despite its Baroque appearance, the **Basílica de la Macarena** is Seville's least historic church. Yet it attracts tourists and pilgrims by the coachload. It was built in the 1940s to house the city's most popular religious image, *María Santísima de la Esperanza Macarena.* Visitors can come around the back of the altar for a close look at the dark-skinned Macarena Virgin, weeping diamond tears. The identity of the artist is disputed, but his Baroque sculpture is the object of a mass cult. Also on show here are the jewels, silversmith's art and embroidered capes associated with the Macarena.

Next door to the basilica, the 13th-century **Iglesia de San Gil** (St. Giles Church) was the original home of the Macarena Virgin. San Gil was badly damaged and looted in the Civil War horrors of 1936, but the church's prime treasure was spared. Just before the violence broke out, one of the parishioners "kidnapped" the Virgin, hiding her in his house until peace returned to Seville.

The arch in front of the basilica, the **Arco de la Macarena,** is a gateway of the old city wall, much changed by Baroque additions. Here begins the best preserved stretch of the ancient city defenses, originated by the Romans and improved on by the Moors. In modern times the wall and its turrets and towers have been restored so earnestly that the perfect ranks of battlements stand out like a set of fluorescent false teeth. Across the street from the wall, a Chinese restaurant has wittily adopted the name *Gran Muralla*—the Great Wall.

Excursions

With Seville as a base, daytrips can take you from mountain to marshland to beach, from ancient history to timeless charm. If you can spare a few days, there are longer excursions to the all-time highlights of Andalusia. Some bus and train connections are quite good, but for maximum flexibility—and to make the most of your time—there's no substitute for a car.

Our suggestions include essential cultural and natural treasures; to vary the pace we add some offbeat stops. There are footnotes to history on the way, and hidden villages so unsophisticated that the local graffiti are written in chalk.

Santiponce and Itálica

Just north of Seville (on the N-630 highway to Mérida), the ancient Roman city of Itálica was the birthplace of two emperors, Trajan and Hadrian. Life was comfortable then, as witness the remains of mansions with magnificent mosaics, and Roman baths, and what's claimed to have been the third largest amphitheatre in the entire empire.

Itálica, near the modern town of Santiponce, was founded in 206 B.C., during the Second Punic War. After several centuries of growth and affluence, Itálica came to mirror the decline and fall of the empire. Nature itself provided the last straw: in 1775 an earthquake bowled over what was left of the ruins.

The **amphitheatre,** which seated 25,000 for gladiatorial contests, has seen better days, but in spite of its rundown condition the design and sheer size can still be appreciated. In recent years international festivals have been held here. The amphitheatre is surrounded by a restful park, shaded by the sort of tall slim pines that evoke Rome itself.

In the 19th century archaeologists began swarming over the remains here and in the nearby Roman residential area, and they've been at it ever since. You'll see them on the town site today, in blue overalls, sifting the shards of Roman amphoræ from the dirt, and dusting off the mosaics. There's plenty of work left for generations to come. The most impressive of the ancient Roman statues from Itálica are on display in Seville's archaeological museum. But on the spot you can appreciate some admirable **59**

mosaic floors, along with the city plan, which includes an efficient sewer system.

The Roman **theatre** was built in the era of Tiberius, taking advantage of a hillside slope. Now it's alongside a modern residential section in Santiponce. The theatre is being restored to its original grandeur, or perhaps moreso, using modern construction techniques.

Another highlight of Santiponce, the **Monastery** of San Isidro del Campo, was founded in 1301 by Alonso Pérez de Guzmán ("the Good"), who is buried within. Outstanding are the retable carved by Martínez Montañes and the Mudéjar cloister. Like many a historic building hereabouts, the monastery is being spruced up for the 1992 anniversary: it's to reopen as a parador.

Carmona

The busy N-IV highway from Seville to Córdoba cuts through a fertile countryside well known to the ancient Romans. Actually, the city of Carmona, 33 kilometres (20 miles) east of Seville, existed long before the Romans arrived; first settled in neolithic times, it was a principal base of the mysterious Tartessians.

Entering Carmo, as the Romans called it, you go through the **Puerta de Sevilla** (Seville Gate), a Roman construction elaborated on by the Moors. It wound up as a modest Alcázar (fortress) rather than a mere gate. Up the hill, the main square, the Plaza de San Fernando, offers some breathing space among the narrow streets, and distinguished official buildings from the 16th and 17th centuries.

Among half a dozen beautifully decorated churches around the town, the Prioral de Santa María (St. Mary's Priory) stands out despite its unimpressive exterior. Enter through a Moorish patio soaked in the scent of orange blossoms and see the fine Gothic vaulting and details within.

At the top of the town, the **Alcázar** del Rey Don Pedro (King Peter's Castle) enjoys unbeatable views of the surrounding agricultural region. Part of the rambling medieval fortress now serves as a parador with all modern conveniences; tourists can breakfast in a basilica-sized dining room.

Beyond the centre of town, to the west, the Roman **Necropolis** (closed Sunday afternoons, Mondays and holidays) encompasses hundreds of tombs and mausoleums at

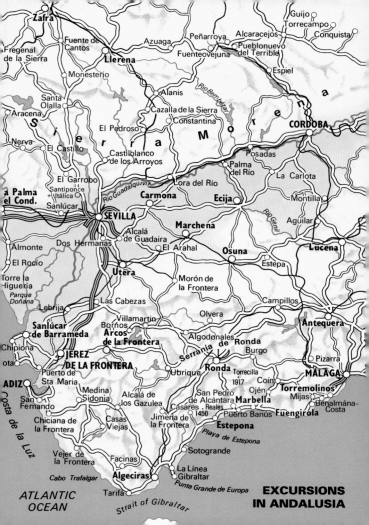

EXCURSIONS IN ANDALUSIA

least 2,000 years old. The Tomb of Servilia is an underground palace of overwhelming grandeur; the complex Elephant Tomb (the first to be excavated) is announced by a statue of an elephant. These funeral chambers were used by priests for rituals to honour the dead. A small museum on the site displays a cross-section of the funerary accessories, sculptures and inscriptions unearthed since the necropolis was discovered in 1868. Across the road, grass covers an unexcavated Roman amphitheatre.

Écija

The local tourist authorities would like you to label Écija *Ciudad del Sol* (Sun City). But the nickname that sticks is "Frying-pan *(Sartén)* of Andalusia". The simple topographical fact is that Écija occupies a depressed site concentrating the hot air; it's far more uncomfortable in summer than Seville. Other than that disadvantage, it's a pleasant small city blooming with tiled church steeples and imposing town houses. Écija is a good place to stop on the way to Córdoba—any time but summer.

Plaza de España, the main square, doesn't win hearts at first sight, but it's an agreeable mix of architectural styles, including a few elegant old buildings. Gossip and parking problems are the main concerns here. Just off the square, the 18th-century Church of Santa María has assembled a so-called archaeology museum in the courtyard. The exhibits go back to Roman times—inscriptions, grinding wheels, vases, mosaics and mostly chipped statues.

The Parish Church of Santiago, reached through a lovely patio, was much rebuilt in Renaissance and Baroque style. The 16th-century main altar is highly prized. The Church of San Juan looks as if an earthquake had spared the steeple but doomed the rest of it. In fact, they may have simply run out of funds, although there was a ground shifting in the 17th century. In the garden you can see the remains of a mosque, which originally occupied this site. The tallest of Écija's 11 towers marks the Church of Santa Cruz, an 18th-century church on the site of the city's main mosque.

Osuna

On the Seville–Málaga highway, the agricultural centre of Osuna remembers a troubled but sometimes glorious history.

The Iberians founded Osuna, which was to be known by a number of names: Urso, Ursona, Orsona and the Arabic Oxuna. After the Romans arrived, the town underwent an awkward interlude. Osuna sided with Pompey the Great in his civil war struggle against Julius Caesar. Pompey lost, and so did Osuna, which became a colony of Caesar.

After five centuries under Moorish control, Osuna was reconquered by Ferdinand III in 1240. The town found greatness in the 16th century, when the dukedom of Osuna was created in 1558 by King Philip II and given to the head of the Knights of Calatrava, Pedro Téllez de Girón. He and subsequent Dukes of Osuna ordered the construction of the city's most monumental buildings, including a number of splendid palaces. They're notable for the use of stonework—the columned doorways, the bas-relief coats of arms. Among the most worthy civic buildings are the Antigua Audiencia (former Law Courts) and the Renaissance and Baroque palaces of various noble families.

The mid-16th-century complex of the Antigua Universidad (former University) stands powerfully at the top of the town. The Iglesia Colegiata (Collegiate Church) counts four saintly paintings by José Ribera among its treasures. The Mausoleo Ducal (Ducal Sepulchre or Pantheon of the Osunas) is as lavish as it sounds.

Córdoba

Two distinct Golden Ages, centuries of political power and cultural attainment, account for Córdoba's glow of greatness. The first big break came under the Romans; the second, even bigger, under the Moors.

The birthplace of the intellectual Seneca family, Córdoba was the capital of Rome's Hispania Ulterior. It became the biggest Roman city on the Iberian peninsula. In the Middle Ages, indigenous Christians and Jews helped Córdoba blossom under Muslim rule as a centre of culture, science and art. By the 10th century, the capital of the caliphate was as big and brilliant as any city in Europe.

After the Reconquest, the Spaniards customarily levelled mosques and built churches atop the rubble. In Córdoba, happily, they spared one of the world's biggest, most beautiful mosques. But they couldn't resist building a cathedral inside it. The result is called the **Mezquita-Catedral.** A high wall surrounds the sacred enclosure. You reach the mosque through the ceremonial forecourt with its fountains and orange and palm trees. Inside, in the half-light, an enchanted forest of hundreds of **columns** seems to extend to infinity. The columns—of marble, onyx, jasper—are topped by arches upon arches, in red and white stripes.

Almost hidden in the middle of these acres of beauty is the **cathedral** itself, a spectacular sequel in Gothic and Baroque styles, rising far above its surroundings. The Emperor Charles V told the sponsors: "You have destroyed some-

thing unique to build something commonplace.''

Southwest of the mosque, on the river, Córdoba's **Alcázar** was actually built by a Christian king, Alfonso XI. There are pleasant patios, Roman statues and mosaics, and terraced gardens.

To absorb the full flavour of Córdoba, there's no substitute for wandering the narrow streets and alleys of the **Barrio de la Judería** (Jewish Quarter), in which a small 14th-century synagogue can still be found. You'll need all your peripheral vision not to miss glimpses of cool, flowered patios, so perfect they seem like show windows for traditional Spanish life.

The **Museo Provincial de Bellas Artes** (Provincial Fine Arts Museum), on the historic Plaza del Potro, contains paintings by old masters like Goya, Murillo, Ribera and Zurburán. It also has the definitive collection of works by the local sculptor Mateo Inurria Lainosa (1867–1924), ranging from a characterful portrait of an ancient Seneca to a heroic mariner to dreamy nudes.

Columbus Country

Many a Spanish town, not least Seville, jealously claims an intimate connection with Christopher Columbus. And the great navigator indeed travelled all over the country from Andalusia to Cataluña. Special men-

Recapturing Córdoba from the Moors, the Spaniards spared this regal mosque, then "improved" it. 65

tion, though, goes to the Río Tinto area around the industrial port city of Huelva for having hosted him *before* he became a celebrity. You can follow his footsteps:

In 1485 Columbus and his son Diego arrived at the Franciscan monastery at **La Rábida.** The prior of the monastery, who shared Columbus's belief in a spherical world, intervened with Ferdinand and Isabella on the explorer's behalf. He also offered endless hospitality while Columbus planned his trip and waited for a word from his sponsors. Monks take visitors around the Mudéjar-style monastery several times a day (except Mondays), so you can visit the cozy chapel where Columbus prayed. It contains two prized works of art, a 15th-century figure of Christ on the Cross and the 14th-century Virgin of the Miracles.

A 20th-century work of sculpture, a giant impression of Columbus at the helm, rises along the waterfront on the road from Huelva to La Rábida, all but overwhelmed by nearby refineries. The monument is the work of Gertrude V. Whitney (1877–1942), the daughter of the tycoon Cornelius Vanderbilt, who also established New York's Whitney Museum.

The pleasant little town of **Palos de la Frontera** anticipated the 500th anniversary of the Columbus adventure by building a broad new boulevard. Palos is where Columbus is said to have stocked up with water before taking off for America. Since then, however, the river has silted up and Palos is surrounded by farmland, mostly producing strawberries. A monument marks the fleet's legendary water source, *La Fontanilla*. Palos also honors, with a marble statue, Martín Alonso Pinzón. A local shipowner and navigator, he helped Columbus with logistics and commanded the *Pinta* on the historic trip.

Columbus recruited other crewmen in the nearby hill town of **Moguer.** It's also the birthplace of the Nobel prize-winning poet, Juan Ramón Jiménez (1881–1958). Pertinent quotations from his works are immortalized on tiles affixed to whitewashed walls all around the town. The 14th-century Convent of Santa Clara, lies behind impregnable-looking crenellated walls.

Two other ports down the coast served as the bases for Columbus's subsequent voyages: Cádiz for the second and fourth outings, Sanlúcar de Barrameda for the third.

Costa de la Luz

The Atlantic-facing shore running from the Portuguese border to the Strait of Gibraltar, the Costa de la Luz (Coast of Light) extends over two provinces, Huelva and Cádiz. Seafaring folk who know the whims and perils of the open ocean share this shore with a relative trickle of tourists. A few of the highlights:

Mazagón has a three-star parador on the edge of town,

Despite concentrated development at Matalascañas, Costa de la Luz beaches remain underpopulated.

but otherwise most of the development in this family resort consists of villas and camp sites. A storm barrier keeps the big waves from crashing onto the town, lying along part of the beach, which is overlooked by a lighthouse. But the total beachfront goes on for more than 12 kilometres (7 miles) of fine golden sand.

An excellent two-lane highway parallels about 25 kilometres of almost empty beaches between Mazagón and the next resort, **Matalascañas.** Bordering on the Doñana National Park, Matalascañas claims to be one of the sunniest beaches in Europe, basking in more than 2,800 hours of sunshine per year. It's so appealing that tourist developments, not always tasteful, have mushroomed. Matalascañas accounts for three-fourths of the hotel capacity in the whole province. There is a diffuse sprawl of red-tile-roofed white villas and "urbanizaciones" along with massive hotel and apartment projects. The buildup seems endless, but, fortunately for those who hate crowds, the beach is endless, too.

A priest rises above the devout throng at the Whitsun pilgrimage in the dusty hamlet of El Rocío.

El Rocío

The edge of a swamp might seem an unpromising setting for a village, but they've built a stylish promenade in El Rocío (meaning "the dew") so you can watch the water birds enjoying the bugs, fish and reeds. The swamp, in this case, is the source of the town's fame.

During the Muslim occupation, the legend says, Christians hid a wood-carved statue of the Virgin in this swamp. With the Reconquest, the statue was recovered, and miraculous powers were soon attributed to it. So a hermitage was built on the spot, and in the second half of the 20th century a big white church in traditional style went up. The faithful come all year round to walk the unpaved streets of the village, buy religious souvenirs, and enter the church to pray before the big glass case containing the Virgin of the Rocío holding a baby Jesus.

Once a year, at Whitsun (Pentecost), El Rocío becomes an Andalusian Mecca, the goal of a vast pilgrimage *(romería).* Well over a million pilgrims descend on the sanctuary in the most folkloric way: on foot, on horseback, by tractor or ox-cart, or by horse-drawn flower-decked wagon. The city of Seville supplies the biggest single contingent, and the Triana district fields an especially strong delegation. They wear festive clothes—flamenco dresses for many of the women—and sleep under the stars along the way. They feast and sing and dance and pray, a blend of activities that the participants find utterly appropriate to the occasion. The real mob scene happens after Sunday night's midnight mass when the Virgin of the Dew is carried through the crowd. All the pilgrims try to get close enough to touch the revered relic, resulting in what elsewhere might be called an unholy scrum.

Doñana National Park

The wilderness of Spain's biggest national park is well worth half a day of your busy holiday. But don't expect a lion-and-elephant safari. The animals you see may be no more exotic than a herd of deer, a couple of wild horses and a flight of flamingos. The lynx, fox and

Wildlife in the Doñana reserve, now a national treasure, was fair
70 *game for medieval royal hunters.*

badger tend to be more inconspicuous.

More extraordinary than the livestock is the environment itself. You'll experience a remarkable ecosystem, a convergence of marshes, Mediterranean-style pine woods, and Lawrence-of-Arabia sand dunes leading to a spectacular de-

serted beach. The ratio of wetlands to dry changes with the season. Conservationists are ready to defend this place, and its 900 species of vegetation, to the last gasp. But the struggle is by no means won. Certain species have already been decimated by pesticides; many flamingos have abandoned drying swampland; and neighbouring tourist developments threaten to overturn the precarious balance of nature.

The national park was founded in 1969 and enlarged nine years later. Including surrounding protected zones, its area is 75,000 hectares (185,000 acres). Up until the late 20th cen-

tury Doñana was little appreciated.

Because of the weird variety of terrain only four-wheel-drive vehicles can be used, and even they sometimes need a tow up a sand-dune. Most visitors are transported in special lofty buses driven by knowledgeable guides. Bouncing or swaying or squishing through thick and thin, sand and swamp, it's a four-hour odyssey covering 80 kilometres (about 50 miles).

Visiting Doñana

It's best to plan far ahead, for the number of visitors is strictly limited and reservations are essential. There are two excursions, morning and afternoon, daily except Monday. They set out from the Reception Centre of El Acebuche, just off the road linking El Rocío and Matalascañas; it's wise to be there half an hour in advance. There is also an information centre at La Rocina, just south of El Rocío.

The telephone number for reservations is (955) 43 04 32. If the situation sounds hopeless, it's worth putting your name on the waiting-list in hopes of last-minute cancellations.

Springtime is by far the best season. In summer be sure to take along drinking water and insect repellant.

You can rent binoculars *(prismáticos)*, though there's little chance to use them as the transporter bounds through the forest or races along the beach. Even so, the naked eye takes in a treasure of sightings, including 250 bird species, permanent or in transit to or from Africa. Among the high-flyers: imperial eagle, crested coot, nightjar and kite.

Jerez

The biggest city in the province of Cádiz, Jerez (population around 175,000) is famous for two thoroughbred lines: old wines and young horses.

To be formal, the full name is Jerez de la Frontera. "Frontera", affixed to the names of a number of towns and villages hereabouts, refers to the medieval frontier between Muslim and Christian Spain. Jerez was under Moorish rule between the 8th and 13th centuries; it was reconquered in 1264 by King Alfonso X (the Wise). And since then: the mosque became the cathedral, the remains of the Alcázar occupy the town's summit, and squeezed between the two is part of the Gonzalez Byass sherry complex.

Sherry, the English name of the locally produced wine, is a

corruption of "Jerez". Some of the many wineries, or *bodegas*, invite the public (weekday mornings only) to see how sherry is blended and aged in dark, aromatic halls. At Pedro Domecq they're proud to show off historic casks; visitors have ranged from the Duke of Wellington to Princess Anne and Plácido Domingo. Gonzalez Byass treats tourists to the tricks of its wine-tippling mice.

As for the horses, the **Real Escuela Andaluza de Arte Ecuestre** (Royal Andalusian School of Equestrian Art) has the smartest, prettiest, lightest-footed mounts you'll ever see. Every Thursday at noon the Jerez riding school puts on a beautifully orchestrated show by horses that strut, goose-step, leap and dance; dogs and cameras are forbidden. The rest of the working week, midday training sessions may be watched. Best of all, try to make it to Jerez for the annual spring horse show.

By way of historical monuments, Jerez can offer the crenelled walls of the Moorish **Alcázar**, now surrounded by gardens and underpinned by a subterranean car park. This 11th-century ruin was the fortress-palace of the Caliph of Seville until it was stormed by Alfonso X. He converted the Alcázar's mosque into a Catholic church.

Down the hill, on the site of the city's principal mosque, the cathedral-style **Colegiata** (Collegiate church) was mostly built in the 16th and 17th centuries. Pigeons fly among the flying buttresses of this unusual church, whose belfry stands like an afterthought across a small street. Atop the cupola, a checkerboard tile dome crowns a tower. Inside the church, appropriately, there's a precious image of *Cristo de la Viña* (Christ of the Vineyards).

Sanlúcar de Barrameda

A wine-lover's pilgrimage to Andalusia might well include a detour to Sanlúcar de Barrameda, less than 25 kilometres (15 miles) northwest of Jerez. Sanlúcar is the home of Manzanilla, a variation on fine sherry much appreciated by enthusiasts of fortified wine aperitifs. They say they can taste the sea breeze in every sip of pale, light Manzanilla. You can learn more during a visit to one of the local *bodegas*.

Aside from its wine industry, Sanlúcar is a fishing port at the junction of the Guadalquivir and the Atlantic. A lengthy **73** sand beach marks the river's last hurrah before the open ocean, with the wilds of Doñana National Park across the way. The beach is the site of horse races during the local festival in August.

The riverfront fishermen's quarter, *Bajo de Guía*, is quaintly authentic, and enhanced by some enticing seafood restaurants. Five centuries ago Sanlúcar was a leading Spanish port, chosen by Columbus as the point of departure for his third journey to America and by Magellan for his round-the-globe expedition. The church of **Nuestra Señora de la O** *(Our Lady of the O)*, dating from the 14th century, has a Mudéjar portal. A castle and two palaces highlight the civil architecture of the town.

Cádiz

The Atlantic Ocean and the city of Cádiz, about 120 kilometres (75 miles) south of Seville, have been inseparable for 3,000 years. The affair began when Phoenician traders from Tyre discovered the strategic shelter of its harbour. They called the port Gadir and soon parlayed Spanish fish and salt into a big fish-curing industry. (To this day Cádiz exports salted fish.)

The old city of Cádiz occupies a fist-shaped peninsula separated from "mainland" Spain by a narrow sandbar; the beaches on the isthmus have been improved, and modern apartment blocks and hotels line the causeway. Cádiz is a port, shipyard and naval base, and a moody place to soak up the salty air of history.

Like many generations of sailors before him, Columbus valued the easy, safe access that Cádiz offered to the Atlantic, and in his days it was headquarters for the Spanish treasure fleets. From Cádiz he sailed on his second and fourth voyages to America, and many treasure-hunters were to follow.

The historical highpoint of local pride was the defiance of 1812. Under siege by Napoleon's forces, Cádiz entertained delegates from around the country to compose a liberal Spanish constitution. The Cortes (the Spanish parliament) met in the **Oratorio de San Felipe Neri,** a domed church in the maze of the old town. You can hardly see the building itself for all the memorial plaques vying for prominence on the façade. Inside is a painting of the Virgin attributed to Murillo.

During the 17th and 18th

centuries Cádiz was readied for any foreseeable attack, with the old town walled and bulwarked. The best relic of these defences is the **Puerta de Tierra** (Land Gate), still guarding entry to the old city via the isthmus from the rest of Spain.

You can't miss the Baroque **cathedral,** overlooking the ocean, with its landmark dome of glazed yellow tiles. The lavish treasury features a monstersized monstrance made of a ton of silver imported from the New World.

One of the most inviting squares interrupting the grid of narrow streets of the old city is the palmy **Plaza de Mina.** Here you'll find, under one roof, the Museum of Archæology and Fine Arts—everything from Phoenician relics to paintings by Murillo and Zurbarán.

White Villages

A luminous legacy of Moorish urban planning is the typical Andalusian hilltop village: narrow twisting streets of whitewashed stone houses with grilled windows and cool patios. There are variations on this stereotype in many parts of southern Spain, but the province of Cádiz probably has the highest concentration of the most appealing white villages.

A historic thread links most of the villages: situated on the border between Muslim and Christian Spain, they were fought over for more than two centuries. Long before that, they had border status because of their location on the farthest frontier of Phoenician influence.

Arcos de la Frontera

Only 30 kilometres (19 miles) east of Jerez, Arcos de la Frontera is one of the classic white villages, perched on a cliffside in the middle of the most heartwarming rural surroundings. Actually, "village" is not quite the word for Arcos, which was honoured as a "city" in 1472, and later "Very Faithful City". The population, on the hilltop and below, is about 30,000.

At the top of the town, the south side of the **Plaza del Cabildo** (Town Hall Square) is bordered by a small promenade on the edge of the precipice. Far below are orchards, olive groves and vineyards prospering under the influence of the snaking Guadalete river.

Progress has doomed the plaza, once a parade ground, to serve as a car park; most local streets are so narrow that twoway traffic, much less parking, is out of the question. On the east side of the square, a three- **75**

Kestrels haunt the cliffs beneath the seemingly impregnable white village of Arcos de la Frontera.

star parador occupies a restored palace, with more overpowering views. Opposite, the **Ayuntamiento** (City Hall) has a grand panelled ceiling in the main hall.

On the north side of the plaza, the 16th-century **Parroquia de Santa María** (St. Mary's Parish Church) is notable for its lavishly carved main altar, chapels and choir and the intricate vaulting of the ceiling. The main façade, which faces west, is categorized as Gothic-Plateresque; it involves swirling sculptural details and bas-reliefs of four rampant lions upholding amphoras, symbolic of this church's official supremacy over its historic rival.

The challenger, the **Parroquia de San Pedro** (St. Peter's Parish Church), clings dramatically to a cliff-edge, possibly

the site of an earlier Moorish fortress. It's a massive Gothic structure with a Baroque façade and belfry and an outstanding 16th-century main altar. As for the feud between the two churches, it simmered for years over the issue of primacy. Finally, early in the 18th century, St. Mary's sent a representative to Rome, on muleback, to plead its case. In 1764, presumably after years of deliberation, Pope Clement XIII ruled that St. Mary's was indeed Highest, Oldest, Most Illustrious and First among the churches of Arcos.

People who don't want to take sides in the feud have several other local churches to choose from. And there are a number of other buildings of historic and architectural interest. But most of the pleasure of Arcos is simply wandering the steep, narrow streets among mansions and cottages, making chance discoveries amidst the beauty of it all.

Beyond Arcos

Eleven kilometres (7 miles) northeast of Arcos, **Bornos** meets the standards of whiteness and charm, but it lacks a hilltop. It's set like a resort town alongside an artificial lake, the Embalse de Bornos, a refreshing parenthesis of the Guadalete river. Bornos is generally a very low-profile town of single-storey white cottages, but one palace stands out—the Palacio de los Ribera (Palace of the Ribera family), retaining a dilapidated grandeur. Alongside, though, the palace gardens (now a public park) are a lush palm-shaded enclave of roses, lilies, and fragrantly flowering bushes and trees. In the local Iglesia de Santo Domingo is a painting attributed to Murillo.

Villamartín, farther along the Guadalete, was founded as recently as 1503, and has the air of a prosperous agricultural centre. The town square has one palm tree at each corner and a fountain in the middle. Storks nest atop the belfry of the 17th-century church, off-white for a change.

In **Olvera,** one of the most spectacularly situated hilltop towns, the only thing higher than the church is the 11th-century fortress, a bunker built atop a spike of stone.

The view from the plaza in front of the big 19th-century neoclassic church is so magnificent that even the local folk congregate there to admire their domain. Olvera is big enough to have a busy business district, yet small enough to retain the "white village" atmosphere, the hillsides covered with seemingly random arrays of tile-roofed houses.

Ronda

Clinging to a clifftop sundered by a deep gorge, Ronda is a strong competitor for the title of Spain's most dramatically sited town. The dizzying emplacement has always appealed to strategists. Under the Moors, Ronda proved impregnable for well over seven centuries.

The **gorge** that cleaves the city plunges 150 metres (nearly 500 feet) down to the surly Guadalevín river. During the Civil War, hundreds of Nationalist sympathizers were hurled to their deaths into the abyss, a tragedy that inspired Hemingway in his novel *For Whom the Bell Tolls*.

For the best prospect of the gorge and the patchwork of fields beyond, catch the view from the Puente Nuevo (New Bridge). It has spanned the ravine for more than two centuries, leading to the **Ciudad,** the old Moorish enclave. Ronda's Moorish kings—and Christian conquerors—used to live in the **Palacio de Mondragón.** The chief mosque survives a street or two away as the church of Santa María la Mayor. The minaret was converted into a bell tower and a Gothic nave was tacked on to the original structure.

Across the chasm again in the newer part of town called Mercadillo, Ronda's neoclassical **Plaza de Toros** (bullring) is one of the oldest in Spain. A Ronda man, Francisco Romero, spelled out the rules of bullfighting in the 18th century.

West from Ronda

A big town bisected by the river of the same name, **Ubrique** is known for its fine leatherwork. (Harnesses and cowboys' chaps used to be the main product, but Ubrique's only industry now turns out the sort of items that tourists buy all over Spain.)

Aside from the souvenir shopping, a couple of sightseeing possibilities are suggested: The 15th-century Iglesia de Nuestra Señora de la O (Church of Our Lady of the O) and the 16th-century Iglesia de San Pedro (St. Peter's Church).

El Bosque means "the woods", and this well-kept white village is surrounded by young forests. Figuring prominently among the local arts and crafts is woodcarving. Behind El Bosque rises a modest but pretty mountain range, the Sierra del Pinar.

Medina Sidonia has a history so distinguished that the local church is a goldmine of artwork. Commanding a crucial salient of countryside, the town flourished as the headquarters of the illustrious Guzmán family, the dukes of Medina Sidonia. The seventh duke entered history as commander of the Spanish Armada in its disastrous encounter with the British in 1588. The Gothic **Iglesia de Santa María la Coronada** (St. Mary's Church), built when the ducal line was established, is almost as big as a cathedral. Start with the thoroughly glorious Baroque retable, so big and intricate that it is said to have taken a team of sculptors more than 30 years to finish. Higher up the hill, cows graze amidst the remnants of the ancient ramparts. They enjoy a gratifying panorama of the fertile hills of Andalusia. In the town below, the noble **Casas Consistoriales,** an arcaded Renaissance city hall, faces the main square.

What to Do

Sightseeing is only part of the story. What to do before, during or after the excursions offers an inviting batch of options: the challenge of shopping, the outdoor sporting life, an entertainment menu satisfying both highbrow and common tastes, the spectacle of bullfighting, the frenzy of flamenco. And if your timing is right, you can plunge into some world-famous festivals.

Shopping

For a quick survey of what Spaniards are buying, browse through the chain department stores—*el Corte Inglés* and *Galerías Preciados*, which are only a few streets apart in central Seville. For orientation, use the multilingual directories posted at the entrances, or go to the main-floor desk dedicated to helping foreign tourists. Unlike local firms, the chain stores stay open bravely through the lunch and siesta break until about 8 in the evening.

Seville has a branch of *Artespaña*, the official network of showplaces for Spanish artisans, at Plaza de la Concordia 2. They stock classy handicrafts,

from artistic ceramics and furniture to a full suit of armour.

But everybody's favourite shopping area is Calle Sierpes and neighbouring streets. Pedestrians often crowd the traffic-free streets, strolling along, cheerfully window-shopping or stopping for a drink. Anything and everything can be bought here, as inconsequential as a souvenir thimble or as pricey as elegant leather or jewellery.

A note about taxes: The Spanish government levies a value added tax (''IVA'') on most items. Overseas tourists can be refunded the IVA they pay on purchases over a stipulated amount, but some paperwork is involved. Shopkeepers, who have the forms, can explain the procedures. The rebate is supposed to catch up with you after you've returned home. (In any case, keep all your shopping receipts handy to show customs.)

Best Buys in Brief

Alcohol. Brandy, sherry, table wines and quaint local liqueurs, among the last of the bargains in Spain, are a good idea for last-minute souvenirs or gifts.

Antiques. Let the buyer beware among the theoretically authentic *antigüedades*: paintings, polychrome sculptures,

Sunday Shopping

Just because all the shops are shut on Sunday doesn't mean shopping fans have to abstain. They can rush out to Seville's wonderful sabbath street markets.

The **Alameda de Hércules** is a Sunday morning carnival of knickknacks and amazing junk... even real antiques. These include paintings, sculptures (some look medieval) and keys and locks that might have come from old castles. Just for fun, look over the historic radios and farm implements, careworn tires, and other second-hand paraphenalia including, literally, kitchen sinks.

In stately **Plaza del Cabildo,** under the arches, the Sunday morning stamp-and-coin market extends beyond philately and numismatism to collectable crystals, used lottery tickets and classic postcards.

The **Plaza de la Alfalfa** animal market is the liveliest Sunday morning date. Canaries of astonishing, perhaps ephemeral colours sing for their lives, hoping a talent scout is in the crowd. (If you don't have a birdcage handy, and don't want to buy one here, the canary man will pack your purchase in a paper bag!) Also up for adoption are puppies of immense charm, turtles and turtle-doves, mice and hamsters, peacocks, and even silkworms, sold with mulberry leaves so you can start your own silk factory.

illuminated medieval psalters, hand-made rugs, furniture, porcelain and crystal. Check the serious dealers in the Santa Cruz district and central Seville, then survey the less predictable offerings at Sunday's Alameda de Hércules flea market or the traditional Thursday bazaar in Calle Feria.

Ceramics. Now that the historic kilns at the Cartuja monastery have gone cold (the British-owned company moved to the outskirts of Seville), Triana is the place to go to find ceramics at the source. And shops all over the city sell traditional plates, pots, pitchers, figurines and ornamental tiles.

Embroidery. In many a village, the women still spend their days at the kind of needlework their grandmothers taught them: handkerchiefs, tablecloths, pillowcases and scarves. And specialist shops in Seville sell mantillas, those lightweight shawls for covering shoulders and sometimes heads... as Spanish as their name.

Fans. Spanish folding fans, **81**

the sort coquettish *señoritas* are supposed to hide behind, are illustrated with hand-painted scenes for every taste. Up-market fans are made of silk and lace.

Fashion. Innovative new designers have propelled Spanish fashion into the big leagues. The most interesting shops are clustered in and around Calle Sierpes. Ready-to-wear children's clothes are charming but expensive.

Flamenco costumes. Seriously, Seville manufactures thousands of flamenco dresses and suits. If you don't need one yourself, think about a child you know. All the accessories are sold in Seville as well, from castanets to guitars.

Foodstuffs. You can take home an aftertaste of Spain, mostly sweet—almonds (roasted or sugar-glazed), dates, figs, marzipan and *turrón* (nougat). And try some of the pastries and sweets confected in the convents of Seville.

Hats. Who knows when you might need a broad-brimmed Andalusian horseman's hat? The woman's model in red would be very chic. Or choose a bullfighter's hat, or a beret from the Basque country.

Ironwork. All around Old Seville you'll be impressed with the wrought-iron ornaments that hide or protect patios and windows: a barrier or a lacy lure, or simply something to beguile. You can buy the same kind of quality in candlesticks, lamps and lanterns.

Jewellery. The medieval Moors brought the silversmith's skills to Andalusia, and the handiwork still shines. You'll find silver and gold rings, bracelets and necklaces, often in sophisticated modern designs.

Leather. At their best, Spanish leather products rate world renown. Whether you're looking for a sturdy wallet or the handbag of a lifetime, you'll find just what you want in Seville. A good choice of fine gloves, belts, coats and shoes as well. Saddlery is a strong point, too: Seville makes everything that goes with horses from harnesses to boots.

Trinkets. The tourists keep coming back for the same old novelties—bullfight posters (with your name as matador), sets of toothpick-sized swords, plastic-lined wineskins, and, irrationally, imitation Mexican sombreros. Seville can sell you pocket-sized toy fighting bulls, flamenco dolls, and models of the Columbus ships.

Azulejos *in Triana ceramic shop proclaim "thanks for your visit".*

Woodwork. Spanish carvers, following a centuries-old tradition, create reproductions of sublime religious statues. Others whittle best-selling Don Quixote statuettes and minifigurines of flamenco dancers. More practically, olive wood is transformed into salad bowls, pepper mills, chess boards and beads.

Sports

Thanks to the climate and the setting, Andalusia has won the loyalty of millions of sports-minded visitors, participants and spectators alike. From top to bottom, the opportunities range from hang-gliding to scuba diving.

Water sports. On the Costas, the leading attraction is clearly swimming, followed by boating, windsurfing, water-skiing and fishing. For endless kilometres of sweeping sandy beaches you can hardly do better than the Costa de la Luz, the closest to Seville—unless the Atlantic rollers put you off. Seville itself has public and private swimming pools; your hotel may have one. For windsurfing, Tarifa, on the breezy Strait of Gibraltar, is a world capital. However, beginners, who might be bowled over at

Tarifa, would do better under the protection of Cádiz Bay.

Boat races. On the river near Seville, you can watch some exciting sailing in April or May when the *Club Náutico* hosts the *Ascenso del Guadalquivir*, a 40-mile race starting at Sanlúcar. Another regatta is scheduled in September or October. And roaring motorboats race on the river in early June. For fans of more basic boat racing, the Andalusian Rowing Federation sponsors the Seville-Betis Regatta every January.

Fishing. Offshore fishing in the Atlantic features grouper, jewfish and more substantial targets—bluefish, tuna and shark. Inland, the Guadalquivir is available for hunters of barbel, bogue and carp. The tourist office can tell you how to get a permit. The trout, for which a supplementary license is required, hang about in the north of the province, in the Rivera del Hueznar around Cazalla and Constantina.

Hunting and shooting. The season generally runs from mid-September to mid-February. In Seville province, hunters bag wild boar, red deer, buck, moufflon, and flying quarry like red-leg partridge and many varieties of duck. There are half a dozen game preserves within 70 kilometres

(43 miles) of Seville. For details about permits and importing arms—it's all very complicated and requires advance planning—check with any Spanish National Tourist Office, or write the national hunting federation: *Federación Española de Caza*, Ortega y Gasset 5, 28006 Madrid.

Horse riding. Andalusia is horse country, and the capital is Jerez, home of Spain's supreme riding school and some of the brightest, most handsome horses anywhere. In Seville, the best horses and riders tend to get together at the Club Pineda, on the Jerez highway. The *Hipódromo de Pineda*, attached to the club, is the scene of colourful racing in autumn and winter. In August the horse racing moves to an unusual setting—the beach at Sanlúcar de Barrameda—for a rollicking three days.

Tennis has a wide following in Spain, with well over a thousand clubs operating. Beyond the club scene, some of the luxury hotels have their own courts.

Golf. Seville's Club Pineda establishment includes a 9-hole golf course. Elsewhere, Andalusia is sprinkled with courses, most of which welcome non-members. The national tourist organization issues a map showing all the country's golf courses with facts about each of them; or consult the Andalusian Golf Federation, Paseo del Pintor Sorolla 34, 29016 Málaga.

Football (soccer) is the most popular spectator sport in Spain. Seville has two teams, Real Betis Balompié and Sevilla Club de Fútbol—for short, Betis and Sevilla. The rivalry is easily as intense as that between Liverpool and Everton or the Chicago Cubs and White Sox. But in Seville the boundaries are socio-economic: the working class tends to support Betis while the upper crust cheers for Sevilla. If you can go to the stadium to see either of the teams playing, you'll be in the thick of some memorable atmosphere.

Entertainment

Playtime in Seville starts early with snacks and drinks, followed by dinner, perhaps a show, and then some dancing and nightcaps, all of which is liable to go on far into the night. Somehow life begins anew early the next morning, cheerful and chipper.

After grazing in a *tapa* bar or two, followed by a late dinner (see Eating Out, page 97), you'll be fuelled for a night of **85** unrestrained merriment. Every kind of diversion is close at hand, from opera to girlie show, from flamenco to disco. All you need is time, money and inexhaustible energy.

Travel agencies organize "Seville-by-Night" tours involving dinner and a quota of drinks along with a big flamenco show. They're handy for those visitors, such as unaccompanied women, who might be reluctant to explore nightlife on their own. Since the package is paid for in advance, unexpected expenses are not a problem. River excursions with dinner and dancing on board are another option.

Seville is well equipped with all the requirements for a tempting nightlife—jazz spots, showy nightclubs, discos, pubs, and even a raunchy red-light district. Tastes in nightspots seem to change overnight; check the listings in leisure publications such as *Revista del Ocio* or *El Giraldillo*. Generally, though, the most sophisticated revellers gravitate to the districts of Los Remedios and Triana.

On a more cultural plane, Seville's own symphony orchestra, the *Bética Filarmónica*, performs at home and away. You may also be able to catch a visiting ensemble or soloist in concert in the special atmosphere of a historic church. Music, dance, theatre and other artistic endeavours take over the city in springtime during a festival called *Cita en Sevilla* (Rendezvous in Seville). In summer the remains of the Roman amphitheatre in Itálica are dusted off for a festival of music, dance and theatre. Back in town, an international festival of music and dance is scheduled in Seville in September. Grand opera is due to take a great leap forward with the opening of Seville's modern Teatro de la Maestranza, the opera house next to the bullring. Spaniards take opera very seriously; consider the contribution of José Carreras, Plácido Domingo, Victoria de los Ángeles, Teresa Berganza and Montserrat Caballé.

Flamenco

Several men in black suits, tieless, wander onto the small stage, strumming guitars or clapping hands in a contagious rhythm. It becomes an epidemic when the frilly-gowned singer/dancer joins them, moving her fingers in the air as sensually as a Siamese dancer, then stamping her heels at a machine gun pace. Even the most reserved, sober, skeptical tourist soon gets into the spirit of flamenco, and unleashes an unsolicited *¡Olé!*.

Flamenco is in its element in Seville. But where the song and dance really comes from is a subject of controversy. "Flamencologists" can take you back to the 14th century, if not Visigothic times. Many of the anguished chants resemble the wailing of Arab music, which must be part of the story. The gypsy influence is also acknowledged. Your best chance to see a flamenco show is at a *tablao flamenco*—it may be tourist-oriented, but the electricity crosses all frontiers of nationality or language.

There are two main groups of songs: The more profound sort, called *cante jondo*, deals with love, death, all the human drama; the singer may seem overcome with grief. The other type, more cheerful and more likely to be performed for tourists, is known as the *cante chico*.

Among the variants are *fandangos, malagueñas, alegrías*, and Seville's one speciality, the *sevillana*, which is altogether bouncier than the average flamenco song. The lilting rhythm follows rigorous rules, and the songs touch on two main themes: local colour, extolling the beauties of Seville and its fiestas, and the inexhaustable subject of love. Seville takes the *sevillana* seriously: youngsters study its finer points in dancing academies around the city.

Fiesta Brava

Say what you will about the bullfight, a dazzling spectacle of violence and beauty, Seville is the place to see the *fiesta brava* at its most authentic. This is the hometown of titanic *toreros* like Pépé Hillo, the 18th-century idol credited with inventing the elegant manœuvre called the Verónica, and 20th-century heroes like Belmonte and Joselito.

Dying young is optional but it adds to a hero's aura. An irascible bull martyred Joselito when he was only 25, whereas his friend Belmonte survived many a goring and lived to be 70. Manolete, Córdoba's favourite son, was killed at 30. Pepe Hillo, author of *The Art of Bullfighting,* wasn't caught until he was 46 years old.

Winning approval from the finicky fans in Seville's bullring of *la Real Maestranza* is the matadorial equivalent of a singer's bringing down the house at Covent Garden or the Met. When it comes to bullfighting, they say in Seville, Madrid is just out in the provinces.

Bullfighting may upset or fascinate or simply confuse **87** you. Is it an art, a spectacle, a metaphysical experience... or ritually choreographed slaughter? Even Spaniards argue the question. Defenders of the *fiesta brava* point out that the doomed bulls live several years longer and incomparably more agreeably on the range in Andalusia than animals grown for food. To assuage critics who condemn the spectacle as barbarous cruelty, it's been suggested that Spain adopt the rules of Portugal, where the bull leaves the ring on its own four feet. But many a devout supporter of tradition would reply, "Over my dead body".

Bullfighting was never meant to be a sport, for no one regards it as a contest between equals; it's one man's wits and dexterity against the brawn and

Candlelit prayers and the torero's "suit of lights" illuminate the core of the character of Seville.

instinct of a specially bred beast nearly 10 times his weight. For the bull, the conclusion is foregone. Yet every time the *torero* enters the ring, he knows his own life is in danger.

The programme typically features three matadors who alternate in fighting a series of six bulls. The *corrida* follows an inflexible scenario. To the accompaniment of a fanfare of trumpets and clarinets, the *matadors* and their teams arrive in fanciful, even effeminate, embroidered costumes. After the opening procession, the first of the afternoon's six bulls enters the ring, thus ushering in the first *tercio* (the first part of the drama's three-act ritual). The fighter sizes up the bull's intelligence and agility and begins to tire him, flaunting a big red-and-yellow *capote*. Next the *picador*, a spearman in Sancho Panza costume, mounted on a well-padded blindfolded horse, lances the bull's shoulder muscles to

weaken the animal and to lower its head.

In the second *tercio*, the *banderilleros* stab long darts between the animal's shoulder blades. Compared to the punishment inflicted by the picador, this is a minor inconvenience for the doomed bull.

In the final, fatal *tercio* the matador taunts the bull with the small, dark-red *muleta* cape, eventually dominating him. Finally, as the panting bull stares at his foe, awaiting the inevitable, the matador unveils his sword and lunges over the bull's horns for the kill.

If the matador's courage or skill has disappointed the audience, he is likely to be sent off in silence or with catcalls. After an exceptional fight he may be awarded an ear, two ears or, rarely, two ears plus the tail of the bull just despatched. The ultimate accolade in Seville is to leave La Maestranza through the Puerta del Príncipe (Prince's Gate), carried on the shoulders of the fans.

Does it all add up to the most savage public nightmare? Or an extemporaneous poem about the mystery of life and death? The argument goes on, and so does the spectacle, between April and October, on the great circle of sand in the bullring of Seville.

Fiestas

Seville loves parties and spectacles, and one way or another the calendar sparkles with festivals and fiestas, religious or hedonistic. If you can't time your visit to coincide with one of the prime events, you still may stumble on a lesser-known fair or celebration, either in Seville or in a nearby town or village.

The year of fiestas begins on January 5, the day Spanish children receive the equivalent of Christmas presents. *La Cabalgata de Reyes Magos* (Festival of the Three Kings) is a parade of floats featuring biblical and fanciful figures in the most extravagant costumes. On this unreservedly happy holiday, tons of sweets rain down on the crowds packing central streets.

Carnaval (which was banned during the Franco years) usually takes place in February, and makes more of an impact in the provincial towns than Seville itself. It's not that the people aren't keen on fun; they're just getting ready for the exertions of Holy Week and the Spring Feria.

Genuine folklore costumes—and smiles—dazzle at fiesta time.

Easter Week

Seville's *Semana Santa* (Holy Week) is one of Europe's biggest, most moving pageants, a week of faith and folklore with a cast of tens of thousands of hooded believers on the march through historic streets. Even tourists who seldom go to church—any church—are swept up in the fervent crush, becoming instant connoisseurs of Baroque religious art, medieval costumes and penitential protocol.

Every spring since the early 16th century, brotherhoods of Seville Catholics have taken to the streets to mark the Passion and Resurrection of Christ.

Not much has changed except for the sheer number of participants, the degree of suffering of the penitents (in modern times no blood is spilled) and the incomparable sumptuousness of today's spectacle. Nowadays the smell of burning candles, incense and jasmine blends with a redolence of frying fish and spluttering popcorn.

Along the fringes of the official solemnity, the atmosphere is downright jolly. The drumrolls or dirges of the marching bands are punctuated by the shouts of vendors of peanuts, lottery tickets and luxury balloons. In fact, you could consider it a round-the-clock street party interrupted occasionally by silence and deep devotion when a sacred image comes into view.

More than 50 brotherhoods (cofradías), originally united not only by faith but by profession or neighbourhood, march in what would be called parades if they didn't proceed at a tortoise pace. Each group of thousands of participants follows its own route, a walk of up to 12 hours; many penitents do it barefoot or carry heavy crosses, or both. All itineraries converge near the Cathedral. And so does the audience.

Over the course of the week the public gets to applaud about a hundred *pasos*—call them floats or portable altars, though neither translation is adequate. A *paso*, a candle-lit life-sized sculptural ensemble on an intricately carved and embellished bier, is most unportable: it takes 40 or 50 very husky men working themselves to exhaustion to carry it on their backs; labour-saving wheels are barred from Seville's Holy Week processions. Most brotherhoods field two *pasos*, the first illustrating an aspect of the events leading up to the crucifixion. The second is an image of the Virgin surrounded by fresh flowers and adorned with jewels, precious metals and priceless needlework. Among these sculptures are greatly adored images like the Virgin of Macarena and Triana's Virgin of Hope, which have cults of their own.

When one of the beloved Virgins is drawn through a narrow old street, cries of *"¡Guapa!"* (What a beauty!) arise, as if it were a film star. When the float stops, a singer on a balcony may launch into a *saeta*, a brief, flamenco-based lament. The melody and tone resemble a muezzin's call to prayer. The words, directed at the Virgin, can combine prayer, praise and sentimentality. The form is so authentic that poets like García Lorca and the Machados have written *saetas*. Others are composed spontaneously.

Manœuvering the multi-ton *pasos* through the twisting streets requires endurance and discipline. The floats are built to swing and sway, with canopies rustling and flapping. Turning a corner, the porters *(costaleros)* have to avoid stepping on each others' feet. Entering or leaving a church the chore is even more delicate, like berthing an ocean liner in a swimming pool. The crowd applauds successful feats. But the sacred load is so heavy that it is rarely moved more than 100 yards without being grounded for a rest period. While the candle-lighters tend their banks of virgin wax candles, the T-shirted porters, heads bound in Moorish-style slave padding, sprawl on the street catching their breath. Each man carries 40 to 60 kilogrammes (88 to 132 pounds), though not the entire route, thanks to extra porters available for relief.

A plaque in Plaza Alfalfa records the death by heart attack on Holy Wednesday, 1986, of one José Portal Navarro of the *cofradía de San Bernardo*. This is the inscription:

*Tú fuiste mi redentor
y yo fui tu costalero;
yo abajo, Tú en el madero,
por amor.*

(You were my Redeemer, and I was your porter; I below, and You on the cross, for love.)

It's the only case of a *costalero* dying from his exertions.

The marchers, most of them in tall conical hats with masked faces, are called *nazarenos*. They carry tall candles that drip an estimated 25 tons of wax onto the streets. Children along the route pester them for drops of wax which they snowball into big souvenirs of Holy Week. Some of the *nazarenos* are children; well-wishers in the crowd offer them so many sweets that they end up distributing the surplus to other children in the crowd.

If you can't make it to Seville for Easter Week, you can see the much-loved icons and *pasos* in their home churches. The images of Christ are wood-carved statues, as much as four centuries old. The images of the Virgin, though, consist of no more than disembodied face and hands, clothed with great pomp from jewelled crown to three-metre-long cape. The Virgins, all with pretty Seville faces, are shown weeping; some shed tears of diamonds. **93**

April Fair

Seville's *Feria de Abril* seems as deeply engrained in local life as the seasons themselves. Yet it's a relatively recent fixture, established in the middle of the 19th century as a royally sanctioned livestock fair. First proposed by local officials with, oddly enough, Basque and Catalan backgrounds, the rustic fair developed into the most Andalusian of celebrations.

The five-day party is scheduled a couple of weeks after

Participating in one of Spain's most colourful pilgrimages, oxen pull wheeled shrine along the way.

Easter when the spring weather is usually impeccable, fit for parasols, not umbrellas. What seems to be the entire population of the city packs the fairgrounds, on the edge of the Los Remedios district. There's not much to do except dress up in folkloric costumes, visit friends, drink sherry and eat *tapas*, ride horseback, sing and dance *sevillanas*, and maybe fall in love.

Most of the eating and drinking takes place in *casetas*, gaily decorated canvas-roofed little houses. Some are big enough to hold a hundred merrymakers. Unfortunately for the casual visitor, you have to be invited: tourists are on the outside looking in.

Important bullfights are scheduled across the river at the Real Maestranza ring during the fair, enforcing a detour on thousands of the celebrants. The number of fairground streets named after famous matadors is a good indication of the importance of bullfighting to the *feria* mood. After the *toros*, it's back to the fair for dinner, and more of the song and dance mode, followed by fireworks.

Not everyone stays awake for five days and five nights, but Seville's spring *feria* inspires almost superhuman endurance.

Corpus Christi

The Thursday after Trinity prompts a religious procession featuring Seville's richest religious treasure, a huge solid silver monstrance by Juan de Arfe, a 16th-century master. Rose petals are strewn across the streets and flowers brighten

balconies along the Corpus Christi parade route.

All week long crowds come to the cathedral to see a unique style of sacred song and stately dance, performed by boys dressed as medieval pages. The talented lads are called the Seises, from the word for six, but now there are 10. They perform only until their voice changes, so there is a constant turnover in the troupe.

The Sunday after Corpus Christi, the Triana district stages its own "Corpus Chico" parade, starting from Santa Ana church. Like most other events in Triana, it's full of life and colour.

Calendar of Events

January	*Cabalgata de Reyes* (Festival of the Three Kings). In Seville, floats and traditional costumed characters recalling the visit of the Wise Men to the Christ Child.
February or March	Pre-Lenten Carnival exuberance in Seville and Cádiz.
March or April	*Semana Santa* (Holy Week). Hooded penitents and revered religious images in solemn processions the week before Easter in Seville.
April	*Feria de Abril* (April Fair). Seville's happiest week: horses and riders, bullfights and flamenco in Andalusia's most colourful fair.
May	*Feria del Caballo* (Horse Fair). In Jerez, horse lovers revel in events from races to carriage competitions.
June	Whitsun *Romería del Rocío*, one of Spain's biggest religious festivals, invades the hamlet of El Rocío. *Corpus Christi*. Religious parade through Seville, performances of the *Seises* choristers in the cathedral.
July and August	Neighbourhoods in Seville celebrate local saints' days with exuberant fiestas. *Festival de Música, Danza y Teatro* in Itálica.
September	*Festival Internacional de Música y Danza*, Seville. *Fiesta de la Vendimia* (Wine Harvest Festival) in Jerez, with parade, bullfights, flamenco and horse events. *Feria de San Mateo*, a rustic get-together in Écija, dates back to the 13th century.

Eating Out

At first glance you might think no one in Seville has time or appetite for a proper meal. But the people you see devouring the morning pastry, the afternoon snack and the early evening appetizers are merely indulging in sideshows; the restaurants, cooking up voluminous lunches and dinners, are jammed.

Many of the local flavours reflect history. You can thank the ancient Romans for the olive oil and wine, and the Moors for the spices. The explorers who followed Columbus brought back tomatoes and potatoes, and Seville's cloistered nuns outdid the Arabs in confecting sweets.

Spanish restaurants are officially graded by forks, not stars. One fork is the lowest grade, five forks the top. Ratings are awarded according to the facilities available, not the quality of the food. The sign of many forks on the door guarantees spotless tablecloths, uniformed waiters, lavish lavatories and high prices—but not necessarily better cooking.

Incidentally, if a restaurant looks frightfully Andalusian, don't assume it's a tourist trap. The locals like it that way, too.

The Timetable

Breakfast can be anytime you like (in hotels it's often 8 to 10 a.m.) but lunch and dinner are startlingly late by the standards of northern Europe or North America. Lunch is unlikely to start before 2 p.m., and Spaniards rarely even think about dinner until 9 p.m.

Breakfast is generally an inconsequential meal, consisting of *café con leche* (half expresso coffee, half hot milk) and a croissant or pastry. Most hotels offer breakfast, though it's not normally included in the price of the room. At neighbourhood bars, where prices are far cheaper, many breakfasters order a *tostada* (toasted roll) with butter or perhaps marmalade or ham. An alternative is *churros*, lengths of fritters to be sugared to taste. Some luxury hotels and *paradores* lay on weighty breakfast buffets of hot and cold foods.

Lunch can be heavy or light, leisurely or rushed, however you want it. If your sightseeing programme is supercharged, you can snack in a café, or sit at the counter of a *cafetería* for a *plato combinado*, one of the set dishes. With time and money to spare, have lunch in a *restaurante*. A *menú del día* (day's special) usually lists three courses at a reasonable set price.

Between meals, **snacks** are ever popular, starting with a slice of cake or a creamy pastry in a *pastelería* or *confitería*. On another plane, specialist bars—characteristic of Seville—feature *tapas*, snacks of infinite variety.

In tourist areas **dinner** is served starting at 8 p.m., though the locals almost never turn up until after 9, and 10 o'clock is standard. Normally menu prices are "all inclusive"—including tax and service charge. However, a tip is still customary.

What to Eat

If Andalusia had to nominate one recipe to represent it in an international culinary contest, the likely winner would be a dish that needs no cooking: *gazpacho*. This "liquid salad" is the perfect refresher on a hot day. The Greeks are said to have devised the prototype for gazpacho, essentially a bread-and-salt soup, as the daily ration of their troops. The Romans brought the idea to southern Spain, adding olive oil. The recipe was embellished in the 16th century by the addition of tomatoes and green peppers from the New World. (To round out the cultural interchange, the name itself comes from the Arabic for "soaked bread".) Nowadays the ingredients also include vinegar, garlic, chopped onion and cucumber, and it's served chilled; you may be offered freshly-diced green pepper and other fresh

Snacks Unlimited

Tapas are snacks to tide you over until the next meal. In Seville they're so good that, if your resistance is low, you might forget all about lunch. *Tapas* are either finger food or items you can impale on a toothpick—anything from marinated olives to garlic-fried mushrooms, from hot meatballs to a cold slice of Spanish omelette, from oysters to *soldaditos de Pavía*, quick-fried chunks of cod.

At peak hours there's a mob scene in bars that specialize in *tapas*, customers fighting for space at the counter, the servers shouting orders, and debris piling up on the floor. Don't hesitate to toss your olive stones, mussel shells and used paper napkins on the floor; if you don't, the waiter will!

The "menu" is often chalked on a blackboard, but you don't have to know the names. Just point to what you want. One helping is called a *porción*; a large serving, suitable for knife-and-fork attention, is known as a *ración*.

vegetables, chopped egg and fried croutons to sprinkle on.

Andalusia's most prized appetizer is *jamón serrano* (highland ham); watch the waiter or chef deftly slice the meat off the bone, discarding any imperfections. Especially renowned is tender Jabugo ham from the mountains of Huelva province, where the pigs dine on acorns.

Many a meal begins with a salad, accenting endive and green olives, or with a plate of cooked vegetables—*judías verdes* (green beans) or *habas* (broad beans) or *espinacas* (spinach). Egg dishes, too, are popular starters. *Huevos a la flamenca* is a baked dish of eggs with tomato, garlic and herbs, usually acocompanied by diced ham or sausage, fresh peas and sweet red pimento.

A moveable feast in Seville is *pescaíto frito*, the local term for quick-fried fish, famed for its light, flaky texture. As in the British tradition of fish and chips, the fried fish here is bought wrapped to "take out", not to be eaten on the spot. If you order a mixed bag (actually, it comes in a paper cone) you may taste hake, whiting, plaice and sardine. Take it to a nearby bar, order some white wine and let these typical treats melt in your mouth.

In restaurants the fish of the day, prepared as elaborately or as simply as you please, might be *lenguado* (sole), *merluza* (hake), *besugo* (sea bream), *atún* (tuna) or *rape* (pronounced *rah*-pay—monkfish or angler-fish). Shellfish is rushed in from the coast—*langosta* (spiny lobster) served hot or cold, or grilled prawns (*gambas* or *cigalas*). If you're squeamish about squid in its ink *(calamares en su tinta)*, try the less daunting, chewy rounds of *calamares fritos*.

Meat-eaters may turn to *ternera a la sevillana*, veal in sherry sauce with green olives, or another local speciality, *cola de toro*, bull's tail in a heavy wine sauce, resembling the Italian *osso bucco*. Another typical Andalusian dish is *riñones al Jerez*, kidneys sautéed in sherry. But steak-lovers from Texas or Argentina are unlikely to rave about the local beef.

Typically, dinner in Seville ends with something sweet, such as *yemas de San Leandro* or *bollitos de Santa Inés*— traditional delicacies produced by local nuns. Andalusia also appeases sweet-toothed fanatics with chewy *turrón* (nougat). For light relief, switch to the bounty of fresh fruits— strawberries, cherries, grapes, peaches or melons. **99**

Wine and Spirits

Andalusia has been producing, and consuming, wine for about 3,000 years. The prehistoric Phoenicians planted the first vines, and the Greeks refined the enterprise. Then came the Romans, with their enthusiasm for an amphora or two of red or white or amber. The industry grew and grew, with only a few interruptions—the scorched-earth policy of the Vandals and the teetotal regime of the Moors (who, in any case, *ate* the grapes). Today Spain has more square miles of vineyards than any other European country. Even an ordinary restaurant's *vino de la casa* (house wine) is well worth trying, and the very special wines are truly splendid.

Most of the Spanish regions produce wine of one sort or another. Among the table wines, the oldest and most vigorously protected *Denominación de Origen* is *Rioja*, from the Ebro valley of northern Spain. If you're looking for local colour,

Huelva has a *Denominación* of its own, and Córdoba and Málaga provinces produce delicious semi-sweet and sweet wines as well as table wines.

But the nation's proudest wine comes from Cádiz province: sherry, the fortified wine from Jerez de la Frontera. It is made by the *solera* method, involving three or four rows of oak aging casks. The bottom row contains the oldest sherry, which is bottled when needed, whereupon the cask is filled

from the one above it, and so on. This means uniform quality instead of single-year vintages. As a light aperitif, try a dry *fino* or a medium dry *amontillado*. A dark, sweet *oloroso* goes well after dinner.

The nearby port of Sanlúcar de Barrameda produces a much-loved wine of its own, resembling sherry, called manzanilla. Its special tang is attributed to the sea air. The light dry manzanilla is a favourite accompaniment to *tapas*.

Lunching on a hot day, it's permissible to dilute your table wine with bubbly mineral water, or else a cheap fizzy lemonade known as *gaseosa* which transforms heavy red wine into an imitation of *sangría*. Real *sangría* is a mixture of red wine, lemon and orange juice, brandy, mineral water, ice and slices of fruit— rather like punch, and probably stronger than you expect. Spain also mass-produces a sparkling wine of the champagne type, called *cava*. Another hotweather idea is beer, good and cheap and served very cold. And there's a choice of fruit juices and international and local soft drinks.

A toast to sherry at its best in a typical Andalusian village inn. **101**

To Help You Order...

Could we have a table? ¿Nos puede dar una mesa?
Do you have a set menu? ¿Tiene un menú del día?

I'd like a/an/some... Quisiera...

beer	**una cerveza**	milk	**leche**
bread	**pan**	mineral water	**agua mineral**
coffee	**un café**	napkin	**una servilleta**
cutlery	**los cubiertos**	potatoes	**patatas**
dessert	**un postre**	rice	**arroz**
fish	**pescado**	salad	**una ensalada**
fruit	**fruta**	sandwich	**un bocadillo**
glass	**un vaso**	sugar	**azúcar**
ice-cream	**un helado**	tea	**un té**
meat	**carne**	(iced) water	**agua (fresca)**
menu	**la carta**	wine	**vino**

...and Read the Menu

aceitunas	olives	**judías**	beans
albóndigas	meat balls	**langosta**	spiny lobster
almejas	baby clams	**langostino**	large prawn
atún	tunny (tuna)	**lomo**	loin
bacalao	codfish	**mariscos**	shellfish
besugo	sea bream	**mejillones**	mussels
boquerones	fresh anchovies	**melocotón**	peach
calamares	squid	**merluza**	hake
callos	tripe	**ostras**	oysters
cangrejo	crab	**pastel**	cake
caracoles	snails	**pimiento**	green pepper
cerdo	pork	**pollo**	chicken
champiñones	mushrooms	**pulpitos**	baby octopus
chorizo	a spicy pork sausage	**queso**	cheese
		salchichón	salami
chuleta	chops	**salmonete**	red mullet
cocido	stew	**salsa**	sauce
cordero	lamb	**ternera**	veal
entremeses	hors-d'œuvre	**tortilla**	omelet
gambas	prawns	**trucha**	trout
jamón	ham	**uvas**	grapes
		verduras	vegetables

BLUEPRINT for a Perfect Trip

How to Get There

For help with timetables, budget and personal requirements, see a reliable travel agent or the Spanish tourist office in your home country well before departure.

BY AIR

Direct daily flights link London and Paris with Seville (a trip of about 2.5 hours). Intercontinental flights, as well as those from other European cities, usually go to Madrid (from which there are eight or more daily non-stop flights to Seville), or to Barcelona (with up to four non-stop connecting flights every day).

Charter flights and package tours

From the U.K. and Ireland: You can choose from a selection of package tours and flight-only arrangements. If possible, shop around; no single travel agent can know of all the options. Many tour operators recommend cancellation insurance: you lose no money if illness or accident forces you to cancel your holiday.

From North America: Seville is one of the stops in popular package tours covering several Spanish cities during a specified time.

An advantageous formula for transatlantic tourists travelling on their own is usually the Advance Booking Charter (ABC) flight or the APEX ticket, payable two to six weeks in advance (depending on the destination). Midweek travel is usually less expensive.

BY ROAD

Toll motorways (expressways) run across France, skirting Paris, to the Spanish border near Biarritz. From there it's clear motorway sailing to Burgos (some 250 km. or 155 miles). The N-I (E5) goes from Burgos to Madrid (approximately 245 km. or 150 miles), whence the N-IV (E5) to Córdoba and Seville (some 540 km. or 335 miles). In time for Expo-92, the N-IV is to be a motorway all the way. Other motorways will greatly improve road links between Seville and other parts of Andalusia.

If some of these distances seem daunting, you can always sleep through the journey by putting yourself and your car on one of the daily overnight trains from either Barcelona or Madrid.

A long-distance car ferry service operates from Plymouth to Santander in northern Spain (a 24-hour cruise); from Santander, follow the N-623 to Burgos and proceed as described above (a total of well over 800 km. or 500 miles).

Good bus service links Seville with all the main Spanish cities.

BY RAIL

Express trains reach Madrid from Paris in as little as 13 hours. From Madrid to Seville there are several trains per day; the fastest now takes six hours. If all goes according to plan, a high-speed train travelling up to 250 kilometres per hour (155 mph) is to link Madrid and Seville for Expo-92.

From Paris to Barcelona takes nearly 12 hours (nearly 10 hours from Geneva). From Barcelona to Seville (via Córdoba) is another 13 hours.

For full information on the range of special tickets available, consult the Spanish Tourist Office, or RENFE (Spanish National Railways), General Agency for Europe, 1–3 Av. Marceau, 75115 Paris, France.

When to Go

It's sunny and hot—often infernally hot—in Seville during the rainless summer. The daily temperature in August averages out at 27 °C (about 81 °F), but the average daily *maximum* temperature is 36 °C (97 °F), and the mercury has been known to hit 49 °C (120 °F). In a word, beware of sunstroke. Or spend your days at the seacoast (an hour's drive from the city), where temperatures are drastically milder.

Clearly, the best time to visit Seville is in spring or autumn. The average daily temperature in May and October is a delightful 19 °C (66 °F). But rain is a far stronger possibility than in summer. In winter it can get cold and damp, but most often it's quite mild—a relief from the rigours of northern Europe; frost is almost unheard of.

Following are average monthly temperatures for Seville.

		J	F	M	A	M	J	J	A	S	O	N	D
Maximum	°F	59	63	69	74	80	90	98	98	90	78	68	60
	°C	15	17	20	24	27	32	36	36	32	26	20	16
Minimum	°F	42	44	48	52	56	63	67	67	64	57	50	44
	°C	6	7	9	11	13	17	20	20	18	14	10	7

*Minimum temperatures are measured just before sunrise, maximum temperatures in the afternoon.

Planning Your Budget

To give you an idea of what to expect, here's a list of some average prices in Spanish pesetas (ptas.). They can only be *approximate,* however, as prices vary from place to place, and inflation in Spain, as elsewhere, creeps relentlessly up. Prices quoted may be subject to a VAT/sales tax (IVA) of either 6 or 12%.

Baby-sitters. 500–800 ptas. per hour.

Camping. *De luxe:* 400 ptas. per person per day, 500 ptas. for a tent or caravan (trailer) or mobilehome. *3rd category:* 275 ptas. per person, 275 ptas. for a tent or caravan. Reductions for children.

Car hire. *Seat Ibiza* 3,200 ptas. per day, 24 ptas. per km., 35,000 ptas. per week with unlimited mileage. *Ford Escort 1.1 L* 4,600 ptas. per day, 41 ptas. per km., 50,000 ptas. per week with unlimited mileage. *Ford Sierra 2.0* (automatic) 9,400 ptas. per day, 83 ptas. per km., 85,000 ptas. per week with unlimited mileage. Add 12% VAT.

Cigarettes. Spanish 60–120 ptas. per packet of 20, imported from 185 ptas.

Entertainment. Bullfight from 2,000 ptas., cinema from 300 ptas., flamenco nightclub (entry and first drink) from 2,500 ptas., discotheque from 1,000 ptas.

Hairdressers. *Woman's* haircut, shampoo and set or blow-dry from 1,500 ptas. *Man's* haircut 600–1,000 ptas.

Hotels (double room with bath). ***** from 20,000 ptas., **** from 15,000 ptas., *** from 8,000 ptas., ** from 3,000 ptas., * from 1,000 ptas.

Meals and drinks. Continental breakfast 300–400 ptas., *plato del día* from 500 ptas., lunch/dinner in good establishment from 1,500 ptas., beer (small bottle or glass) 60–100 ptas., coffee 50–100 ptas., Spanish brandy 100 ptas., soft drinks from 80 ptas.

Shopping bag. Loaf of bread 40–150 ptas., 250 grams of butter 190 ptas., dozen eggs from 190 ptas., 1 kilo of steak 1,100–1,350 ptas., 250 grams of coffee 300 ptas., 100 grams of instant coffee 390 ptas., 1 litre of fruit juice 170 ptas., bottle of wine from 150 ptas.

Sports. *Golf* (per day) green fee from 7,000 ptas., caddie fee 2,000 ptas. *Tennis* court fee 600–1000 ptas. per hour, instruction from 2,000 ptas. per hour. *Windsurfing* from 1,500 ptas. per hour. *Horseback riding* 1,200 ptas. per hour.

Taxi. Meters start at 80 ptas. Long distances negotiable.

An A–Z Summary of Practical Information and Facts

> Listed after some basic entries is the appropriate Spanish translation, usually in the singular, plus a number of phrases that should help you when seeking assistance.

ACCOMMODATION *(alojamiento)*. Spanish hotels are classified in star categories, from one-star frugality to five-star luxury. *Hostales* and *pensiones* range from one to three stars. At the one-star level, rooms rarely have bathrooms. Five stars guarantee all the comforts of world-class hotels, from haute cuisine restaurants to shopping facilities.

All hotels, *hostales* and *pensiones* are required by law to have a rates chart at the reception desk and the price of each room posted behind the door. Check that the VAT *(IVA)* government tax is included. This varies from 6 to 15 %. In Seville the hotel rates go up by more than 50 % during Holy Week and the April Feria. Even so, they are jammed, so reservations far in advance are essential.

When you check into your hotel, you may have to leave your passport at the reception desk. It will be given back to you the next morning.

Hostales and **Hotel-Residencias.** These are modest hotels, often without a restaurant, although optional full board may be offered. In Seville's old city some of them capture the authentic atmosphere better than more expensive places.

Pensiones. Small boarding houses, with few amenities. They may provide full board.

Fondas. Inns, small and clean and unpretentious.

Paradores. Mostly off the beaten track, these state-run hotels may occupy converted castles, palaces or monasteries.

Youth hostels *(albergue de juventud)*. Despite the name, there is no age limit, although theoretically people under 26 have priority. There is usually an 11 p.m. curfew. Note that the Spanish word *hostal* (see above) does not mean "youth hostel".

I'd like a double/single room.

Quisiera una habitación doble/ sencilla.

with/without bath/shower

con/sin baño/ducha

A **AIRPORT**. Seville Airport (SVQ) is 12 km (about 7.5 miles) east of the city. The facilities are being expanded for Expo-92 to accommodate more than three times the present capacity of passengers. (Málaga and Jerez airports are also being upgraded.) There are luggage trolleys, a money exchange office, a telephone centre, restaurant, café and shops, including a duty-free shop for departing passengers. A bus service links the airport and central Seville but there are only about ten trips per day. The bus ride takes between 30 and 40 minutes. Taxis, usually found in abundance at the airport, do the trip more quickly.

C **CAMPING**. There are three year-round camp sites within 15 kilometres (about 10 miles) of the centre of Seville, and many elsewhere in Andalusia. Facilities vary, according to the category, but electricity and running water are standard. Some of the bigger establishments have a comprehensive range of amenities—shops, small playgrounds for children, restaurants, swimming pools and launderettes. For a complete list and map of approved campsites all over Spain, consult the Spanish National Tourist Office in your country or write to the Federación Española de Empresarios de Camping y Centros de Vacaciones:

General Oraa, 52, 2º D, 28006 Madrid; tel. (91) 262 99 94.

CAR RENTAL (coches de alquiler). See also DRIVING. You can choose from among a dozen or more international and local car-hire firms, with offices at the airport or in town. The local firms often charge less than the big names. Ask for any available seasonal deals.

The law requires you to have an International Driving Permit, but in practice your national licence will probably suffice. (A translation in Spanish could prove useful in case of an accident.)

Many agencies set a minimum age for car hire at 21. A deposit as well as an advance payment for the estimated rental charge is generally required, but holders of major credit cards are normally exempt from this. A tax of 12 % is normally added to the total charge. Third-party insurance is automatically included; full collision coverage is optional.

CLOTHING. Between June and September, the days are always hot, but take a jacket or cardigan in case of a cool evening or over-enthusiastic air-conditioning. During the rest of the year evenings can be chilly, though frost even in deepest winter is rare.

Don't forget comfortable walking shoes. As for formality, Spain is relaxed about clothing these days, but you should dress soberly when visiting churches.

COMMUNICATIONS

Post Office *(Correo)*. Seville's main post office (Avenida de la Constitución, 22) is undergoing a massive restoration in readiness for Expo-92. Meanwhile branch post offices are sharing the load. The office next to the San Bernardo railway station is handling parcel post. Post office hours are normally 9 a.m. to 1 p.m., Monday to Friday.

Stamps are also on sale from tobacconists *(tabacos)*. Postboxes *(buzón)*, often British-style pillar boxes, are yellow with two horizontal red stripes; red ones are for express mail only. If you see a mailbox marked *extranjero*, it's reserved for foreign-destination letters.

In Spain the postal service is separate from the telephone system, so you cannot usually make telephone calls from a post office.

Telegrams. You can send telegrams at the post office or by telephone. The number is 422 20 00 for telegrams to Spanish destinations and 422 68 60 for the international service. Or ask your hotel receptionist to process it for you. (Hotels also handle fax communications.) Night letters or night-rate telegrams *(telegrama de noche)* are delivered the following morning and cost much less than full-rate messages.

Telephone *(teléfono)*. You can make international calls from public telephones. These booths are equipped with instructions in English. Go armed with a hoard of 5, 25 and 50 peseta coins. There are also operator-assisted long-distance telephone installations where tourists congregate. And private shops operate telephone offices where you can dial directly and pay the owner the sum shown on the meter after the call.

Telephone calls abroad are cheaper between 10 p.m. and 8 a.m. There is no cheap weekend rate.

To make a direct international call from Spain, dial 07 and wait for a high-pitched dialling tone. Dial the country code, followed by the area code, omitting the initial 0, then the telephone number.

A stamp for this letter/ postcard, please.	**Por favor, un sello para esta carta/tarjeta postal.**
express/airmail	**urgente/vía aérea**

COMPLAINTS. Tourism is Spain's leading industry and the government takes complaints from tourists very seriously. Most disputes are due to misunderstandings and language problems and should not be exaggerated. All hotels and restaurants are required by law to have complaint forms *(Hoja Oficial de Reclamación)* available.

C

Police and Guardia Civil stations have forms in English for complaints. Any local tourist office should be able to direct you to the appropriate quarter. In Seville this would be the office of Sanidad, Consumo y Bienestar Social in Plaza de la Encarnación, tel. 421 82 87.

CONSULATES *(consulado)*. If you run into trouble with authorities, consult your consulate for advice. You should know, though, that a consul cannot pay your hotel, medical or any other bills, give legal advice, get you a job or a work permit, pay for travel tickets (except in very special circumstances) or get you out of jail.

Canada: Avenida Constitución 30; tel. 422 94 13.

Great Britain: Plaza Nueva 8; tel. 422 88 75.

U.S.A.: Paseo de las Delicias 7 (in Maria Luisa Park); tel. 423 18 85.

For other countries, check the telephone directory alphabetical section under "Consulado".

Where is the American/British/ Canadian consulate?	**¿Dónde está el consulado ameri- cano/británico/canadiense?**
It's very urgent.	**Es muy urgente.**

CONVERSION CHARTS. For fluid measures, see page 114. Spain uses the metric system.

Temperature

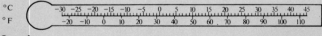

Length

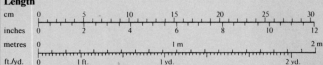

Weight

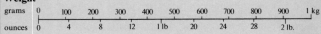

COURTESIES. In spite of all the recent, drastic changes in Spanish society, politeness and simple courtesies still matter. A handshake on greeting and leaving is normal. Always begin any conversation, whether with a friend, a shop girl, taxi-driver, policeman or telephone operator with a *buenos días* (good morning) or *buenas tardes* (good afternoon). Always say *adiós* (goodbye) or, at night, *buenas noches* when leaving. All requests should begin with *por favor* (please). And don't try to rush Spaniards. Haste is considered unseemly.

CRIME AND THEFT. Seville is notorious for the vigour and resourcefulness of its minor criminals. Muggings and petty larceny are all too common, as the authorities and ordinary citizens warn tourists, so it's only sensible to take precautions:

- Secure passport, traveller's cheques, credit cards and reserves of cash in a money belt or, better still, entrust valuables to hotel safe-deposit boxes.
- Dress unostentatiously and forswear jewellery—especially gold.
- Always lock your car and stow any possessions out of sight in the boot (trunk).
- Never leave anything of value visible in your car, even while driving.
- In the event of a robbery, offer no resistance—some thieves are armed.

I want to report a theft.   **Ha habido un robo.**

CUSTOMS, ENTRY AND EXIT REGULATIONS. Nationals of Britain, Eire, the U.S., Canada, Australia and New Zealand need only a valid passport to visit Spain, and even this requirement is waived for the British, who may show a "visitor's passport". A national identity card is sufficient for citizens of other Western European countries.

Although visitors to Spain are not currently subject to any health requirements, it is always wise to check with a travel agent before departure in case any inoculation certificates are needed.

Currency restrictions. There are no restrictions on the amount of local and foreign currency brought into the country. Non-residents of Spain must declare sums exceeding 100,000 pesetas in local currency or 500,000 pesetas worth of foreign currency on entry, to avoid possible problems on departure.

A maximum of 100,000 pesetas may be exported in local currency. Permission must be obtained from the monetary authorities for larger sums.

C **Duty-free.** Here's what you can carry into Spain duty-free and, upon your return home, into your own country.

Into:	Cigarettes		Cigars		Tobacco	Spirits	Wine
Spain 1)	300	or	75	or	350 g.	1.5 l. and 5 l.	
2)	200	or	50	or	250 g.	1 l. or 2 l.	
Australia	200	or	250 g. or		250 g.	1 l. or 1 l.	
Canada	200	and	50	and	900 g.	1.1 l. or 1.1 l.	
Eire	200	or	50	or	250 g.	1 l. and 2 l.	
N.Zealand	200	or	50	or	250 g.	1.1 l. and 4.5 l.	
S.Africa	400	and	50	and	250 g.	1 l. and 2 l.	
U.K.	200	or	50	or	250 g.	1 l. and 2 l.	
U.S.A.	200	and	100	and	3)	1 l. or 1 l.	

1) Visitors arriving from EEC countries.
2) Visitors arriving from other countries.
3) A reasonable quantity.

Reimbursement of sales tax. The major stores can help foreign visitors from outside the European Community get refunds on the VAT/sales tax (IVA) paid on larger purchases. Complete a form at the shop, have it stamped and signed, and on departure present it at the customs, along with the goods. The rebate will be forwarded to you at home.

I have nothing to declare.	**No tengo nada que declarar.**
It's for my personal use.	**Es para mi uso personal.**

D **DRIVING IN SPAIN**

Entering Spain. To bring your car into Spain you should have:

- International Driving Permit, or a legalized and certified translation of your home licence. (Not obligatory for most West Europeans but recommended in case of difficulties.)
- Car registration papers.
- Green Card (an extension to your regular insurance policy, making it valid for foreign countries. (Advised but not obligatory.)

With your certificate of insurance it's strongly recommended that you carry a bail bond. If you should injure someone in an accident in Spain, you could be imprisoned while the accident is being investigated. This bond would bail you out. Apply to your automobile association or insurance company.

A nationality sticker must be displayed prominently on the back of your car. If your car is right-hand drive, you must have the headlights adjusted, or have anti-dazzle strips on them. Spanish law requires you to carry a complete set of spare bulbs.

Drivers and front-seat passengers must wear seat belts when driving outside towns. Motorcycle riders and their passengers are required to wear crash helmets.

You must have a red reflective warning triangle available in case of an accident when driving on motorways (expressways).

Driving conditions. Drive on the right, overtake (pass) on the left. Spanish drivers often use their horns when passing other vehicles. Lorry drivers (truckers) are usually helpful, blinking their right turn indicator to let you know it's safe to overtake them. As in France, the car coming from the right has priority.

Speed Limits. On international expressways: 120 km/h; on highways: 90 or 100 km/h (depending on the width of the highway); in town or residential areas: 60 km/h.

Motorways *(autopista/autovía).* Spain's motorways are mainly concentrated in the north and east. But as the fateful year 1992 approaches, new superhighways are changing the face of Seville and Andalusia in general. On *autopistas* a toll *(peaje)* is charged. *Autovías* are toll free.

Parking. Parking is difficult in the narrow streets of central Seville. Coin machines on the streets sell tickets entitling the buyer to parking time; the ticket should be displayed inside the windscreen. In some areas human "parking meters", officially recognized or otherwise, attempt to coordinate the situation. Desperate parkers often climb pavements or abandon their cars in obviously unsuitable middle-of-the-road places. The takeaway service known as the *grúa* tows some of the offenders to the pound. For the record, in Spain it's forbidden to park the car facing oncoming traffic. If all this puts you off, patronize one of the underground car parks.

Traffic police. The Traffic Civil Guard *(Guardia Civil de Tráfico)* patrols the highways. Although they are courteous and quick to help anyone in trouble, the police are severe on lawbreakers. Fines are payable on the spot.

D **Accidents.** In case of accident, dial the police emergency number, 091. Avoid admitting guilt or signing any document that you do not understand.

Fuel and oil. Service stations are plentiful, particularly in tourist zones, but it's a good idea to keep an eye on the fuel gauge when you're heading for deserted areas.

Fuel is theoretically available in super (97 octane), normal (92 octane), unleaded (95 octane) and diesel. But not every station carries the full range. It is customary to give the attendant a coin or two as a tip.

Fluid measures

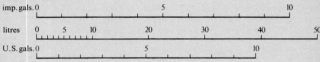

Breakdowns. If you have a breakdown on the motorway, use one of the strategically positioned emergency telephones to call for help. Spare parts are most readily available for Spanish-built cars. For some other makes, spares may be difficult to find.

Road signs. Most signs regulating traffic are the standard symbols used throughout Europe. But you may encounter these written signs:

¡Alto!	Halt!
Aparcamiento	Parking
Autopista (de peaje)	(Toll) motorway (expressway)
Cede el paso	Give way (Yield)
Cruce peligroso	Dangerous crossroads
Cuidado	Caution
Curva peligrosa	Dangerous bend
Despacio	Slow
Desprendimientos	Landslides
Desviación	Diversion (Detour)
Escuela	School
Grúa	Tow-away zone
¡Pare!	Stop!
Peligro	Danger
Puesto de socorro	First-aid post
Salida (de camiones)	(Lorry/Truck) exit

(International) driving licence	**Carné de conducir (internacional)**	**D**
car registration papers	**permiso de circulación**	
Green Card	**Carta verde**	

Are we on the right road for …?	**¿Es ésta la carretera hacia …?**
Full tank, please.	**Lleno, por favor.**
normal/super/unleaded	**normal/super/sin plomo**
I've had a breakdown.	**Mi coche se ha estropeado.**
There's been an accident.	**Ha habido un accidente.**

DRUGS. The official Spanish attitude to soft drugs has changed several times in the post-Franco years; it is currently an offence to possess them. (In student bars especially this may seem hard to believe.) As for hard drugs, the *división especial antidroga* (the Spanish drug squad) is very harsh on foreigners who deal and indulge.

ELECTRIC CURRENT *(corriente eléctrica)*. Although 220-volt A.C. **E** is becoming standard, older installations of 110 and 125 volts can still be found. Check before plugging in. Visitors from North America will need a transformer unless they have dual-voltage travel appliances.

What's the voltage—125 or 220?	**¿Cuál es el voltaje—ciento veinticinco (125) o doscientos veinte (220)?**
an adaptor/a battery	**un adaptador/una pila**

EMERGENCIES *(urgencia)*. Your hotel desk-clerk or a taxi driver—not to mention the nearest policeman—can be of great help in an emergency. If you have a real crisis, dial the police: **091**.
　　The Fire Brigade answers to **080**.

Careful!	**¡Cuidado!**
Fire!	**¡Fuego!**
Help!	**¡Socorro!**
Police!	**¡Policía!**
Stop!	**¡Deténgase!**
Stop thief!	**¡Al ladrón!**

FIRE *(incendio)*. Forest fires are a real menace in hot, dry Andalusia, **F** so be very careful not to throw your cigarette butts and matches away anywhere. If you are camping, make sure your fire is completely extinguished before you move on.

G **GUIDES and INTERPRETERS** *(guía; intérprete)*. The local tourist office, your hotel or a travel agency can refer you to qualified guides and interpreters should you wish a personally directed tour or help with business negotiations.

H **HAIRDRESSERS and BARBERS** *(peluquería; barbería)*. You may have to look down the side streets to find a barber in Seville; red-and-white striped barber poles are not the custom here. Some hotels have their own salons, where the standard is generally very good. You may see much lower prices displayed in the windows of independent salons. Prices vary widely according to the class of the establishment.

haircut	**corte**
shampoo and set	**lavado y marcado**
blow-dry	**modelado**
a colour rinse/dye	**champú colorante/tinte**

HEALTH and MEDICAL CARE. If you already have a health-insurance policy, make sure that it covers you while abroad. Otherwise, take out a policy at your insurance company, automobile association or travel agency. The Spanish tourist insurance, ASTES, covers doctor's fees and hospital treatment in the event of accident or illness.

Visitors from EEC countries with corresponding health-insurance facilities are entitled to medical and hospital treatment under the Spanish social security system.

For minor ailments, visit the local first-aid post *(ambulatorio* or *permanencia)*.

Farmacias (chemist's shops, drugstores) are usually open during normal shopping hours. After hours in Seville, many are open until 10 p.m. and several are open all night for emergencies. The addresses are posted in all other pharmacy windows and published in the newspapers.

As a sensible precaution, take a basic kit of adhesive plaster, antiseptic cream, aspirin, etc., plus an adequate supply of any prescribed medicines.

Where is the nearest (all-night) pharmacy?	**¿Dónde está la farmacia (de guardia) más cercana?**
I need a doctor/dentist.	**Necesito un médico/dentista.**
I've a pain here.	**Me duele aquí.**

116

sunburn	**quemadura del sol**
sunstroke	**una insolación**
an upset stomach	**molestias de estómago**
insect bite	**una picadura de insecto**

HOURS OF OPENING. See also COMMUNICATIONS and MONEY MATTERS. Although the grand old Spanish custom of the siesta is under attack in industrious northern Spain, Andalusia still believes in the afternoon nap—or at least a very long lunch hour. Office hours in Seville, built around the ample midday break, are generally from 9 a.m. to 1:30 p.m. and from 4:30 to 7 p.m.; Saturdays from 9 a.m. to 1:30 p.m.

Shops are open from 9:30 to 1:30 and from 4 to 8 p.m. Monday to Friday, and until 1:30 or 2 p.m. on Saturdays. Department stores, though, tend to work nonstop from 10 a.m. to 8 p.m., Monday to Saturday.

Museum hours vary, but your best bet is the morning session between 10 a.m. and 1 p.m. Some re-open in the afternoon. Monday is closing day.

LANGUAGE. After Chinese and English, the most widely spoken international language in the world is Spanish. In Andalusia you may find the slurred local accent a bit difficult to understand. A distinctive feature of Seville speech is that the letters *c* and *z* are pronounced "s", without the Castilian lisp. Seville slang includes many gypsy words. In tourist areas, hotel and restaurant staff are proud to display their knowledge of English, German or French.

Good morning/Good day	**Buenos días**
Good afternoon/Good evening	**Buenas tardes**
Good night	**Buenas noches**
Please	**Por favor**
Thank you	**Gracias**
You're welcome	**De nada**
Goodbye	**Adiós**

The Berlitz phrase book, SPANISH FOR TRAVELLERS, covers most situations you are likely to encounter in your travels in Spain. The Berlitz Spanish-English/English-Spanish pocket dictionary contains some 12,500 concepts, plus a menu-reader supplement.

Do you speak English?	**¿Habla usted inglés?**

L **LAUNDRY and DRY-CLEANING.** Most hotels handle laundry and dry-cleaning, but they usually charge more than an outside laundry *(lavandería)* or a dry-cleaners *(tintorería)*. For greater savings, you can try a do-it-yourself launderette *(launderama)*.

I want these clothes cleaned/ washed.	**Quiero que limpien/laven esta ropa.**
When will it be ready?	**¿Cuándo estará lista?**
I must have this for tomorrow morning.	**La necesito para mañana por la mañana.**

LOST PROPERTY *(objetos perdidos)*. The first thing to do when you discover you've lost something is obviously to retrace your steps. If nothing comes to light, report the loss to the nearest police station. Details of objects left on trains should be reported to the station master at the destination. Seville's bus company has a lost and found office at

Calle Diego de Riaño 2, tel. 442 00 11, ext. 211.

I've lost my wallet/handbag/ passport.	**He perdido mi cartera/bolso/ pasaporte.**

M **MAPS.** The Seville tourist office issues free maps of the city pinpointing the big hotels and historical monuments. Commercial mapmakers also produce city maps of various sizes, sold in bookstores or at newsstands. For the roads of Andalusia, the Michelin map is complete and up-to-date.

The maps in this guide were prepared by Falk-Verlag, Hamburg.

MONEY MATTERS

Currency. The monetary unit of Spain is the *peseta* (abbreviated *pta.*).
   Coins: 1, 2, 5, 10, 25, 50, 100, 200, 500 pesetas.
   Banknotes: 500, 1,000, 2,000, 5,000, 10,000 pesetas.

Banking hours. In winter, banks generally open from 9 a.m. to 2 p.m., and Saturdays until 1 p.m. However, some banks stay open until 4:30 p.m. Monday to Thursday. Summer hours are reduced: Monday to Friday from 9 a.m. to 1 p.m., and no Saturday openings. Outside normal banking hours, travel agencies and other businesses displaying a *cambio* sign will change foreign currency into pesetas. The exchange rate is a bit less favourable than in the banks. Hotels, too, can change money, but at a less advantageous rate.

Credit cards. Generally, all internationally recog‐
accepted by Spanish hotels, principal restaurants an

Eurocheques. Most hotels and department stores

Traveller's cheques. In tourist areas, some shops
and travel agencies accept them, but you are likely
exchange rate at a national or regional bank. When cashing
cheques, you have to show your passport.

Paying cash. Although many shops and bars will accept payment in
sterling or dollars, you're better off paying in pesetas, for you'll
invariably receive a poor exchange rate on the spot.

Prices. The days when holiday-makers revelled in Spanish bargains
are long gone, but the country remains reasonably competitive in the
European price league. In the realm of eating, drinking and smoking,
Spain still provides indisputable value for money. To give you an idea
of what things cost, a cross-section of prices is listed on page 106.

I want to change some pounds/ dollars.	**Quiero cambiar libras/dólares.**
Do you accept traveller's cheques?	**¿Acepta usted cheques de viaje?**
Can I pay with this credit card?	**¿Puedo pagar con esta tarjeta de crédito?**
How much is this?	**¿Cuánto vale?**

NEWSPAPERS and MAGAZINES *(periódico; revista)*. Where tour‐
ists congregate you can buy most European and British newspapers
and magazines on the day of publication. U.S. magazines are avail‐
able, as well as the Paris-based *International Herald Tribune*.

For listings of events in Seville, see the locally edited dailies *ABC* or
El Correo de Andalucía. A giveaway monthly brochure, *El Giraldillo*,
prints all the entertainment possibilities.

PHOTOGRAPHY. Only one problem: Andalusia's white-walled vil‐
lages and shining seas fool the electronic eyes on automatic cameras,
tending to darken pictures. Read your camera instruction book in
advance, or have a chat with a camera dealer and show him your
equipment.

Most of the popular international film brands and sizes are avail‐
able in local shops, though the prices are generally higher than in the

Europe or North America. Cheaper are the Spanish films
, and Valca in black and white, and Negracolor in colour. Shops
ring one-hour developing service are now common in central
ville.

In some churches and museums, photography, or the use of flash,
is forbidden.

I'd like some film for this camera	**Quisiera un carrete para esta máquina.**
black and white film	**carrete en blanco y negro**
colour-slide film	**carrete de diapositivas**
for colour prints	**carrete para película en color**
May I take a picture?	**¿Puedo sacar una foto?**

POLICE *(policía).* There are three police forces in Spain: the *Policía Municipal*, attached to the town hall; the *Cuerpo Nacional de Policía*, a national anti-crime unit; and the *Guardia Civil*, the national police, who patrol highways as well as towns. The famous patent-leather hats, worn by the *Guardia Civil* since 1859, are being phased out in favour of more practical headgear, except for use on special occasions.

If you need police assistance, you can call on any one of the three forces. Spanish police are efficient, strict and particularly courteous to foreign visitors.

Where's the police station?	**¿Dónde está la comisaría?**

PUBLIC HOLIDAYS *(fiesta)*

January 1	*Año Nuevo*	New Year's Day
January 6	*Epifanía*	Epiphany
February 28	*Día de Andalucía*	Andalusia Day
March 19	*San José*	St. Joseph's Day
May 1	*Día del Trabajo*	Labour Day
July 25	*Santiago Apóstol*	St. James's Day
August 15	*Asunción*	Assumption
October 12	*Día de la Hispanidad*	Discovery of America Day (Columbus Day)
November 1	*Todos los Santos*	All Saints' Day
December 6	*Día de la Constitución Española*	Constitution Day
December 25	*Navidad*	Christmas Day

Movable dates:	*Jueves Santo*	Maundy Thursday
	Viernes Santo	Good Friday
	Corpus Christi	Corpus Christi
	Inmaculada Concepción	Immaculate Conception (normally December 8)

RADIO and TV *(radio; televisión)*. Reception at night is usually good enough to allow listeners to tune in to most European countries on medium-wave portables. Stations like the BBC World Service and Voice of America are heard on short-wave at various hours.

Spain has two national television channels plus regional networks and privately operated stations. Many hotels receive satellite programmes in English, French, Italian and German.

RELIGIOUS SERVICES. Most of Seville's historic churches are open for services several times a day. The cathedral schedules five masses on Sunday between 8 a.m. and 1:30 p.m. In addition to the Roman Catholic churches, serving the overwhelming majority of the population, several Protestant denominations are represented. There are no foreign-language services.

TIME DIFFERENCES. Spain follows Central European Time (Greenwich Mean Time plus one hour). From the last Sunday in March to the last Sunday of September, clocks are put one hour ahead for summer time (GMT + 2).

Summer time chart:

New York	London	**Spain**	Jo'burg	Sydney	Auckland
6 a.m.	11 a.m.	**noon**	noon	8 p.m.	10 p.m.

What time is it?   **¿Qué hora es?**

TIPPING. Since a service charge is normally included in hotel and restaurant bills, tipping is not obligatory. However, it's appropriate to tip waiters, bellboys, filling station attendants, bullfight ushers, etc., for their services. The chart gives some general suggestions on what's appropriate:

T

Porter, per bag	minimum 200 ptas.
Maid, for extra services	100–200 ptas.
Lavatory attendant	25–50 ptas.
Waiter	10 % (optional)
Taxi driver	10 %
Hairdresser	10 %
Tour guide	10 %

Keep the change. **Déjalo para usted.**

TOILETS. The rich Spanish language offers several expressions for "toilets": *aseos, servicios, W.C., water* and *retretes*. The first two are more commonly used. Toilet doors are distinguished by a "C" for *caballeros* (gentlemen) or an "S" for *señoras* (ladies) or by a variety of pictographs.

Public toilets are to be found in most large Spanish towns, but rarely in villages. However, just about every bar and restaurant has a toilet available for public use. It's considered polite to buy a coffee or a glass of wine if you drop in specifically to use the conveniences. Or try asking at a hotel.

Where are the toilets? **¿Dónde están los servicios?**

TOURIST INFORMATION OFFICES *(oficina de turismo)*. Spain maintains tourist offices in many countries. They can supply a wide range of brochures and maps on the towns and regions of Spain. If you visit one you can consult a copy of the master directory of all hotels in Spain, listing facilities and rates.

Australia: International House, Suite 44, 104 Bathurst St., P.O. Box A-675, 2000 Sydney NSW; tel. (02) 264 79 66.

Canada: 60 Bloor St. West, Suite 201, Toronto, Ont. M5W 3B8; tel. (416) 961 31 31.

United Kingdom: 57, St. James's St., London SW1A 1LD; tel. (071) 499 0901.

United States: Water Tower Place, Suite 915 East, 845 North Michigan Ave., Chicago, IL 60611; tel. (312) 944-0216/230-9025.

United States: The Galleria Suite 480a, 5085 Westheimer Rd.,
Houston, TX 77056; tel. (713) 840-7411-13.
8383 Wilshire Blvd., Suite 960, Beverly Hills,
CA 90211; tel. (213) 658-7188-93.
665 Fifth Ave., New York, NY 10022;
tel. (212) 759-8822.

On the spot there are tourist offices in most Spanish towns, normally
open from 9 a.m. to 1 p.m. and again from 4 to 7 p.m. They have free
maps, brochures and advice in English.

Seville: Avda. de la Constitución, 21; tel. 422 14 04.
Paseo de las Delicias s/n (at Glorieta de los Marineros
Voluntarios); tel. 423 44 65.

Cádiz: Calderón de la Barca, 1; (956) 21 13 13.

Córdoba: Plaza Judá Leví; tel. (957) 29 07 40.

Jerez: Alameda Cristina, 7; tel. (956) 33 11 50.

Where is the tourist office?   **¿Dónde está la oficina de
turismo?**

TRANSPORT

Trains. The Spanish railway network is operated by RENFE *(Red
Nacional de los Ferrocarriles Españoles)*. While local trains are slow,
long distance services, especially the *Talgo* and *TER*, are fast and reasonably punctual. First-class coaches are comfortable; second-class,
adequate. Tickets can be purchased at travel agencies as well as at railway stations. Seat reservations are obligatory on most Spanish trains.

Talgo, Intercity, Electrotren, Ter, Tren Estrella	Luxury, first and second classes; supplementary charge over regular fare
Expreso, Rápido	Long-distance expresses, stopping at main stations only; supplementary charge
Omnibus, Tranvía, Automotor	Local trains, with frequent stops, usually second class only
Auto Expreso	Car train
coche cama	Sleeping-car with 1-, 2- or 3-bed compartments, washing facilities

123

T

| coche comedor | Dining-car |
| litera | Sleeping-berth car *(couchette)* with blankets, sheets and pillows |

RENFE offers a 5-day classic train tour leaving twice weekly: the Al-Andaluz Express, which runs luxuriously though Córdoba, Granada, Málaga and Seville.

The situation in Seville is complex. There are two main-line stations: Plaza de Armas (formerly Estación de Córdoba) and San Bernardo (also known as Estación de Cádiz), and Madrid trains use one or the other unpredictably. But in time for Expo-92 all services are to be consolidated in the new Santa Justa Station.

RENFE information: tel. 44141 11.

Long-distance buses. Comfortable coaches link Seville with most Spanish towns and some foreign destinations. Most companies share the central bus station, Prado de San Sebastián 1; tel. 44171 11. Other inter-city lines operate from Calle Segura 18 and Calle Arenal 7.

Local buses. The orange buses of TUSSAM (Transportes Urbanos de Sevilla S.A.M.) operate on more than 30 different city routes, but to ease congestion in the historic centre of Seville the bus stops are unusually far apart. Maps of the routes are posted at almost all bus stops. If you plan to do much travelling by bus, buy a Bonobus (nearly half-price 10-trip ticket) at a TUSSAM office or a tobacco shop. Insert the Bonobus ticket in the machine just behind the driver and it is stamped and returned.

Taxis. You can hail a taxi on the street or go to a taxi rank or ask for one by telephone. If a taxi is free a sign, *"libre"*, appears in the right windscreen; if it's not free, an *"ocupado"* sign is shown. The fare is indicated on the meter, but extra charges, such as an out-of-town supplement, may be added.

Radiotaxi: tel. 458 00 00
Teletaxi: tel. 462 22 22

A ticket to...	**Un billete para**
single (one-way)	**ida**
return (round-trip)	**ida y vuelta**
first/second class	**primera/segunda clase**
Would you tell me when to get off?	**¿Podría indicarme cuándo tengo que bajar?**

WATER *(agua)*. If you're particularly sensitive to a change in water, you may want to order the bottled variety, as the Spaniards themselves do. It comes in two versions: still water (non-carbonated) is *sin gas*; fizzy (carbonated) is *con gas*.

a bottle of mineral water   **una botella de agua mineral**

SOME USEFUL EXPRESSIONS

yes/no	**sí/no**
please/thank you	**por favor/gracias**
excuse me/ you're welcome	**perdone/de nada**
where/when/how	**dónde/cuándo/cómo**
how long/how far	**cuánto tiempo/a qué distancia**
yesterday/today/tomorrow	**ayer/hoy/mañana**
day/week/month/year	**día/semana/mes/año**
left/right	**izquierda/derecha**
up/down	**arriba/abajo**
good/bad	**bueno/malo**
big/small	**grande/pequeño**
cheap/expensive	**barato/caro**
hot/cold	**caliente/frío**
old/new	**viejo/nuevo**
open/closed	**abierto/cerrado**
here/there	**aquí/allí**
free (vacant)/occupied	**libre/ocupado**
early/late	**temprano/tarde**
What does this mean?	**¿Qué quiere decir esto?**
I don't understand.	**No comprendo.**
Waiter!/Waitress!	**¡Camarero!/¡Camarera!**

DAYS OF THE WEEK

Sunday	**domingo**	Thursday	**jueves**
Monday	**lunes**	Friday	**viernes**
Tuesday	**martes**	Saturday	**sábado**
Wednesday	**miércoles**		

Index

An asterix (*) next to a page number indicates a map reference. Where there is more than one set of page references, the one in bold type refers to the main entry. For index to Practical Information, see inside front cover.

INDEX

Selection of Seville Hotels and Restaurants

Where to start? Choosing a hotel or restaurant in an unfamiliar city can be daunting. The sheer sprawl of Seville adds to the confusion: do you want to stay, or dine, near the airport or in the historic centre of the city or in a fashionable suburb? To help you find your way, we have selected a representative cross-section of the establishments that frequent visitors and local sources recommend. We've tried to take into account the differing requirements of budget holidaymakers and un-restrained businessmen, of conservative and adventurous travellers.

Be warned that Seville hotel prices go up by more than 50 per cent during Holy Week and the April Fair, in spite of which rooms are very hard to find at the last moment. In any season it's wise to make advance reservations for all hotels and the better restaurants (and check on closing days). Hotel and restaurant prices include a service charge, but a value-added tax (IVA) of 6 to 12% will also automatically be added to the bill.

In the addresses, the five-digit code is for mail. The last digits of the code (01 to 15) pinpoint the postal district in which the establishment is located. Check our map on page 28.

HOTELS

HIGHER PRICED
(above ptas. 10,000)

Alfonso XIII
San Fernando 2
41004 Sevilla
Tel. 422 28 50
130 rooms, 19 suites
*In a class by itself. A sumptuous
local landmark for more than
60 years, attracting visiting kings
and celebrities.*

Doña María
Don Remondo 19
41004 Sevilla
Tel. 422 49 90
61 rooms
*Wonderful site facing Giralda
tower; intimate atmosphere.*

Gran Hotel Lar
Plaza de Carmen Benítez 3
41003 Sevilla
Tel. 441 03 61
137 rooms
*Modern hotel just beyond the
historic centre; restaurant.*

Husa Sevilla
Pagés del Corro 90
41010 Sevilla
Tel. 434 24 12
128 rooms
*Modern drive-in hotel in Triana
district. Convention rooms,
restaurant, cafeteria, garage.*

Inglaterra
Plaza Nueva 7
41001 Sevilla
Tel. 422 49 70
120 rooms
*In city centre, opposite City Hall;
restaurant, garage.*

Macarena Sol
San Juan de Ribera 2
41009 Sevilla
Tel. 437 57 00
327 rooms
*Restaurants, pool, garage, meeting
rooms.*

Meliá Sevilla
Doctor Pedro de Castro 1
41004 Sevilla
Tel. 442 26 11
366 rooms
*Just beyond María Luisa park;
congress facilities, restaurants.*

Pasarela
Avenida de la Borbolla 11
41004 Sevilla
Tel. 441 55 11
82 rooms
*Cafeteria, garage, sauna,
gymnasium.*

Porta Coeli
Avenida Eduardo Dato 49
41018 Sevilla
Tel. 457 00 40
243 rooms
*Convention halls, restaurant,
cafeteria, swimming pool, garden,
parking.*

Sol Lebreros
Luis Morales 2
41005 Sevilla
Tel. 457 94 00
439 rooms
*In Nervión. Restaurant, cafeteria,
pool, sauna, shops.*

Tryp Colón
Canalejas 1
41001 Sevilla
Tel. 422 29 00
204 rooms and 14 suites
*Impeccably restored luxury
hotel near bullring. Lavish lobby,
restaurant, tavern.*

MEDIUM-PRICED
(ptas. 6,000-10,000)

Alcázar
Menendez Pelayo 10
41004 Sevilla
Tel. 441 20 11
116 rooms
*Restaurant, snack-bar,
air-conditioning.*

América
Plaza del Duque
41002 Sevilla
Tel. 422 09 51
100 rooms
*Modern hotel in shopping district.
Big bright cafeteria.*

Bécquer
Reyes Católicos 4
41001 Sevilla
Tel. 422 89 00
126 rooms
*Modern hotel with efficient,
courteous service.*

Corregidor
Morgado 17
41003 Sevilla
Tel. 438 51 11
69 rooms

*Typical patioed Andalusian
building. Quiet location.*

Don Paco
Pza Padre Jerónimo de Córdoba 4
41003 Sevilla
Tel. 422 49 31
220 rooms
*Central location. Restaurant, pub,
garage.*

Fernando III
San José 21
41004 Sevilla
Tel. 421 73 07
156 rooms
*Modern hotel with pool, solarium,
garage.*

Giralda
Sierra Nevada 3
41003 Sevilla
Tel. 441 66 61
107 rooms
*In a private little street
off busy Calle de Recaredo.
Buffet-restaurant.*

Monte Carmelo
Turia 9
41011 Sevilla
Tel. 427 90 00
68 rooms
*Near the river in Los Remedios.
Garage.*

Murillo
Lope de Rueda 7-9
41004 Sevilla
Tel. 421 60 95
61 rooms
*Typically Spanish atmosphere
in pedestrians-only street
in Santa Cruz district.*

Reyes Católicos
Gravina 57
41001 Sevilla
Tel. 421 12 00
26 rooms
Small air-conditioned hotel.

Virgin de los Reyes
Avenida Luis Montoto 129
41007 Sevilla
Tel. 457 66 10
80 rooms
*In modern shopping district
of Nervión. Garage.*

LOWER PRICED
(below ptas. 6,000)

Internacional
Águilas 17
41003 Sevilla
Tel. 421 32 07
26 rooms
*Near lively Plaza de la Alfalfa.
Garage.*

La Rábida
Castelar 24
41001 Sevilla
Tel. 422 09 60
100 rooms
*Old-fashioned charm, on a quiet
but central street.*

Montecarlo
Gravina 51
41001 Sevilla
Tel. 421 75 01
25 rooms
Off Reyes Católicos, calm.

Puerta de Triana
Reyes Católicos 5
41001 Sevilla
Tel. 421 54 04
*Economical, central hotel near the
bullring.*

Sevilla
Daóiz 5
41003 Sevilla
Tel. 438 41 61
35 rooms
*Charming remodelled old building
in restful yet central location.*

Simon
García de Vinuesa 19
41001 Sevilla
Tel. 422 66 60
48 rooms
*A touch of the 18th-century, a few
steps from the cathedral.*

RESTAURANTS

(Graded according to the price
of a typical three-course meal)

HIGHER-PRICED
(above ptas. 4,000)

Albahaca, La
Plaza de Santa Cruz 12
41004 Sevilla
Tel. 422 07 14
*Andalusian specialities and
international cuisine in a high-
ceilinged old mansion—or on the
terrace.*

Antares
Genaro Parladé 7
41013 Sevilla
Tel. 462 75 51
Beyond María Luisa Park,
a stronghold of sophisticated
Basque cuisine.

Figon del Cabildo
Plaza del Cabildo
41001 Sevilla
Tel. 422 01 17
Elegant, expensive international
and Spanish cuisine in a quiet
corner near the Cathedral.

Isla, La
Arfe 25
41001 Sevilla
Tel. 421 26 31
Wholesome food, elaborately
prepared. Specialities from all
over Spain.

Maitres
República Argentina 54
41011 Sevilla
Tel. 445 68 80
Classy cooking in fashionable Los
Remedios.

Oriza
San Fernando 41
41004 Sevilla
Tel. 421 29 90
Luxury-class Basque and in-
ternational cuisine.

Ox's
Betis 61
41010 Sevilla
Tel. 427 95 85
Basque specialities along with
roast meat and fish.

Rio Grande
Betis s/n
41010 Sevilla
Tel. 427 39 56
Glorious view of the Golden
Tower, Andalusian specialities.

San Marco
Cuna 6
41004 Sevilla
Tel. 421 24 40
Inventive cuisine in a historic old
house in Seville's heart.

MEDIUM-PRICED
(ptas. 3,000-4,000)

Asador Jugopan
San Eloy 42
41001 Sevilla
Tel. 456 06 29
Broiled meat specialities, cheerful
decor, central.

Bacalao, El
Plaza Ponce de Léon 15
41003 Sevilla
Tel. 421 66 70
An offbeat menu in an offbeat
location: the speciality is cod
(bacalao) in all its many styles.

Barca de Don Raimundo, La
Placentines 25
41004 Sevilla
Tel. 456 04 91
Elaborate maritime decor, fresh
fish. Next to the Giralda tower.

Bodegón El Riojano
Virgin de las Montañas 12
41011 Sevilla
Tel. 445 06 82
Andalusian dishes in the atmo-
sphere of an old inn.

Casa Robles
Alvarez Quintero 58
41004 Sevilla
Tel. 421 31 50
Spanish and Andalusian
specialities.

Corral del Agua
Callejon del Agua 6
41004 Sevilla
Tel. 422 07 14
Very original recipes served in a
splendid outdoor setting, alongside
the Alcázar wall.

Cueva, La
Rodrigo Caro 18
41004 Sevilla
Tel. 421 31 43
Seafood and lamb specialities
and outdoor dining in Plaza
Doña Elvira.

Don Carlos
General Polavieja 18
41004 Sevilla
Tel. 422 59 79
Andalusian decor and cuisine.

Enrique Becerra
Gamazo 2
41001 Sevilla
Tel. 421 30 49
Wholesome cooking in a setting
that combines historic-rustic and
elegant decors.

Giraldillo, El
Plaza Virgin de los Reyes 2
41004 Sevilla
Tel. 421 45 25
Facing Cathedral, with Sevillan
decor—inevitably touristy.

Hostería del Laurel
Plaza de los Venerables 5
41004 Sevilla
Tel. 422 02 95
A happily cluttered atmosphere,
with hams and strings of garlic
hanging from the ceiling.

Judería, La
Cano y Cueto 13
41004 Sevilla
Tel. 441 20 52
Pleasant Andalusian decor.
Gourmet versions of familiar fish,
seafood and meat dishes.

Luna Parque
Avenida María Luisa 1
41013 Sevilla
Tel. 423 37 20
Garden setting for Andalusian
specialities. Flamenco shows
Friday and Saturday nights.

Llorens
Pastor y Landero 19
41001 Sevilla
Tel. 422 81 27
Opposite Arenal Market, a
modest bar fronts a serious
restaurant.

Mesón Castellano
Jovellanos 6
41004 Sevilla
Tel. 422 57 21
A lively, bistro-style Castillian
restaurant.

Mesón Don Raimundo
Argote de Molina 26
41004 Sevilla
Tel. 422 33 55
A 17th-century convent trans-
formed into an Andalusian
restaurant.

Piletas, Las
Marqués de Paradas 28
41001 Sevilla
Tel. 422 04 04
Cheerful premises shared by a
tapas bar, a cafeteria and a
neighbourhood restaurant.

Raza, La
Avenida Isabel la Católica 2
41004 Sevilla
Tel. 423 20 24
Inside María Luisa Park, a
perfect setting for indoor and
outdoor dining.

San Francisco
Plaza San Francisco 10
41004 Sevilla
Tel. 422 20 56
A historic Seville house is the
dignified setting for cosmopolitan
cuisine.

LOWER-PRICED
(below ptas. 3,000)

Alcázares, Los
Miguel de Mañara 10
41004 Sevilla
Tel. 421 31 03
Andalusian and other Spanish
specialities in a key tourist
location next to the Alcázar.

Modesto
Cano y Cueto 5
41004 Sevilla
Tel. 441 68 11
Outdoor dining, strong on sea-
food.

Solomillo
Santas Patronas 3
41001 Sevilla
Tel. 422 22 09
Good value in meat and fish,
friendly service.

Tartesos
Canalejas 12
41001 Sevilla
Tel. 421 47 94
Small, homey restaurant with
azulejo-tiled walls. Emphasis on
seafood.

Tres Reyes, Los
Reyes Católicos 9
41001 Sevilla
Tel. 421 15 89
Tapas bar on the ground floor,
small restaurant upstairs with
simple fare.

Vegas, Las
Alemanes 7
41004 Sevilla
Tel. 421 31 45
Paella and fresh fish in a small
restaurant or, in season, at side-
walk tables.

Victoria Eugenia
Plaza de Villasís 1
41003 Sevilla
Tel. 422 74 59
Cheery atmosphere and an
eclectic menu in a popular spot
crucially located at La Campana.